KAWAII
UNDERWATER
WORLD

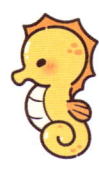  

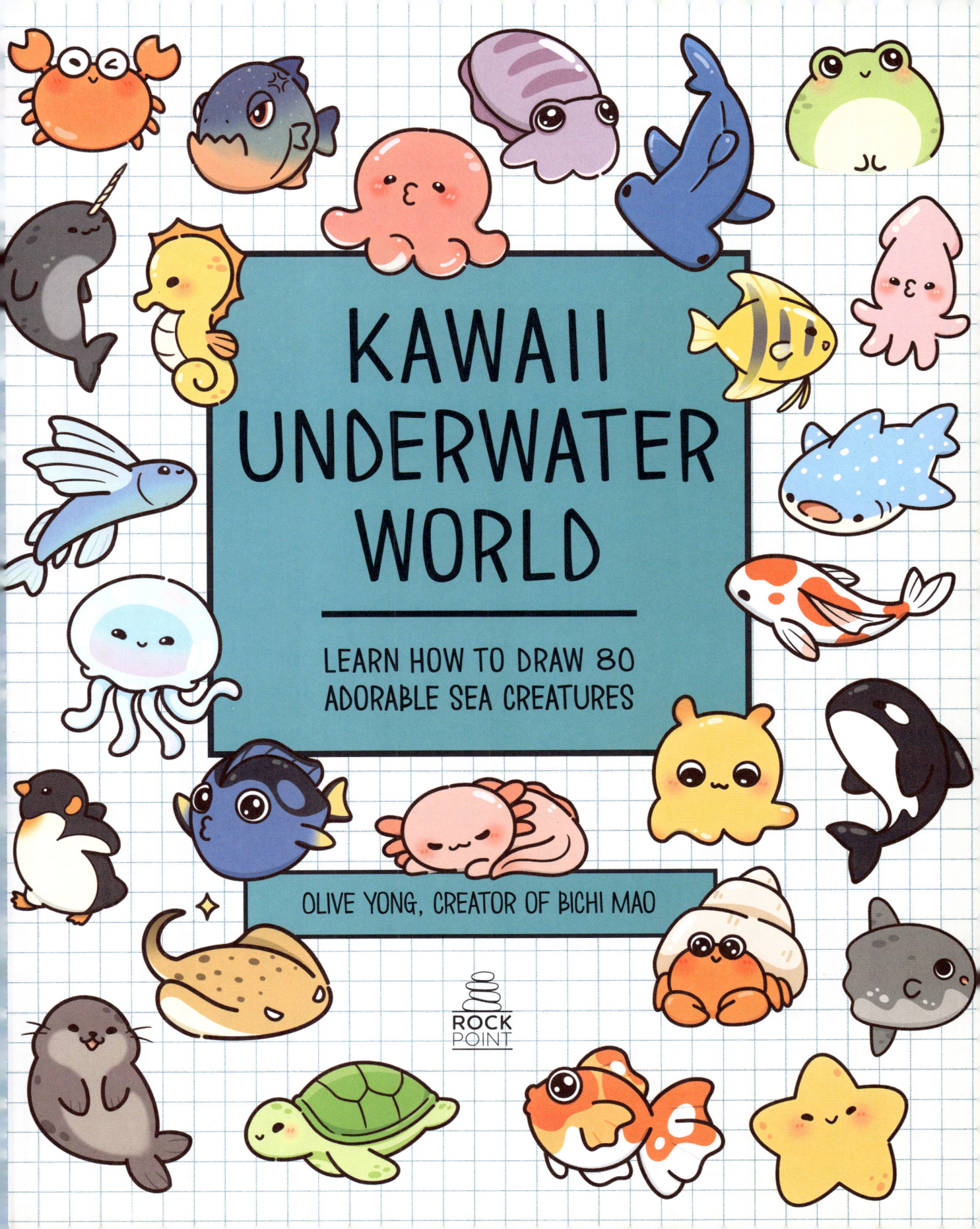

KAWAII UNDERWATER WORLD

LEARN HOW TO DRAW 80 ADORABLE SEA CREATURES

OLIVE YONG, CREATOR OF BICHI MAO

ROCK POINT

First published in 2025 by Rock Point, an imprint of The Quarto Group,
142 West 36th Street, 4th Floor, New York, NY 10018, USA
T (212) 779-4972 www.Quarto.com

Rock Point titles are also available at discount for retail, wholesale, promotional and bulk purchase.
For details, contact the Special Sales Manager by email at specialsales@quarto.com or by mail at
The Quarto Group, Attn: Special Sales Manager, 100 Cummings Center Suite, 265D, Beverly, MA 01915, USA.

10 9 8 7 6 5 4 3 2 1

ISBN: 978-1-57715-518-8

Digital edition published in 2025
eISBN: 978-1-57715-519-5

Library of Congress Cataloging-in-Publication Data

Names: Yong, Olive, author.
Title: Kawaii underwater world : learn how to draw 80 adorable sea creatures /
    Olive Yong, creator of Bichi Mao.
Description: New York, NY : Rock Point, 2025. | Summary: "Learn how to draw
    adorable aquatic creatures through 100 step-by-step tutorials in Kawaii
    Underwater World"-- Provided by publisher.
Identifiers: LCCN 2024061561 (print) | LCCN 2024061562 (ebook) | ISBN
    9781577155188 (paperback) | ISBN 9781577155195 (ebook)
Subjects: LCSH: Drawing--Technique. | Marine animals in art.
Classification: LCC NC781 .Y66 2025 (print) | LCC NC781 (ebook) | DDC
    743.6--dc23/eng/20250127
LC record available at https://lccn.loc.gov/2024061561
LC ebook record available at https://lccn.loc.gov/2024061562

Publisher: Rage Kindelsperger
Creative Director: Laura Drew
Editorial Director: Erin Canning
Managing Editor: Cara Donaldson
Editor: Sarah O'Connor
Cover and Interior Design: Kim Winscher

Printed in China

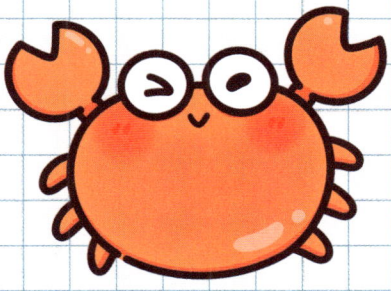

I am truly blessed and grateful to Quarto Publishing Group for once again entrusting me with such an incredible opportunity. Their guidance and dedication have been instrumental in bringing this book to life. This book is dedicated to my Niko Studio Team and my cofounder, Wee Lim, whose inspiration and hard work have enabled me to fully focus on creating this work. To my family and friends, who have always supported my passion for art and believed in me. To my partner, who has been endlessly patient, supportive, and encouraging throughout my journey. To all my Bichi Mao readers, who bring joy to my work by enjoying it and sharing it with the world. To my editor, Erin, and the team at The Quarto Group, for this wonderful opportunity and for guiding me through the publication of my seventh book. Lastly, I am grateful to myself for not giving up and for continuing to push forward. As W. Clement Stone once said, "Aim for the moon. If you miss, you may hit a star."

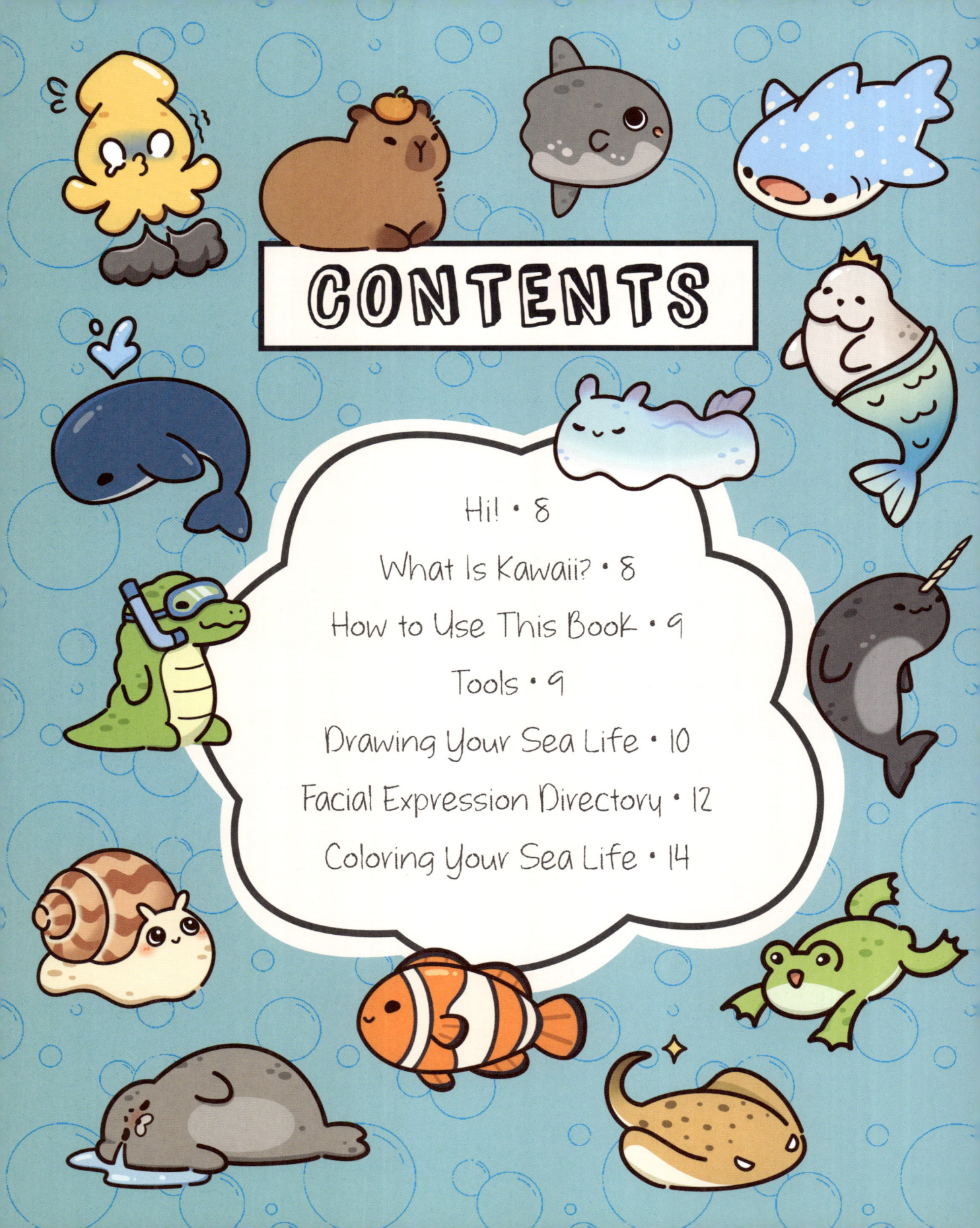

CONTENTS

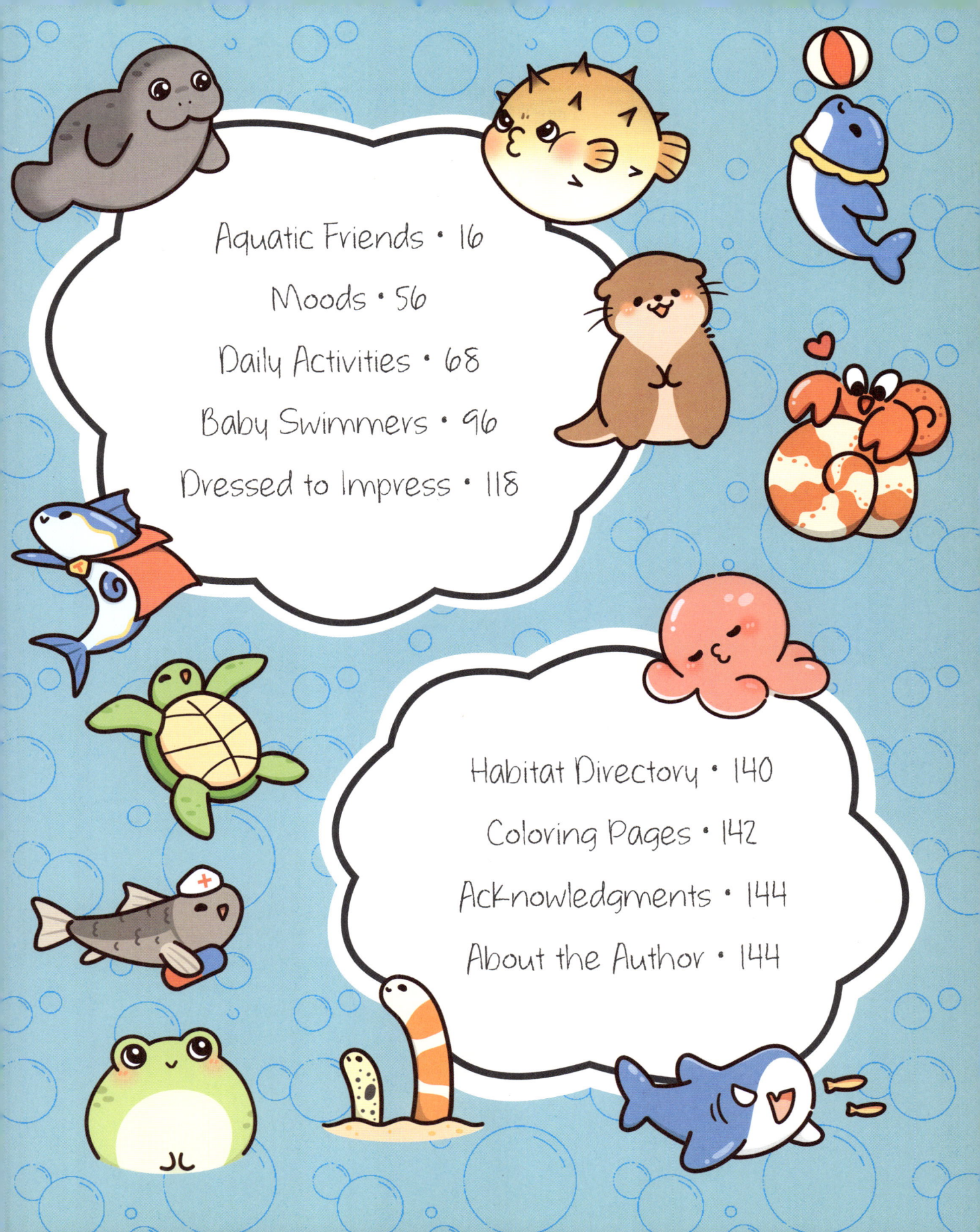

HI!

My name is Olive Yong, and I'm a self-taught artist from Malaysia. Drawing has always been a passion of mine, but it was in June 2019 that I first ventured into digital art. I began sharing my creations across social media platforms under the brand name Bichi Mao, never expecting that humble start to lead to such incredible opportunities. It's been a whirlwind journey, and I'm truly grateful for the blessings that have come my way. Holding my seventh published book now feels like a dream come true.

My publications with Quarto Publishing Group began with *Kawaii Kitties: Learn How to Draw 75 Cats in All Their Glory*, followed by *Kawaii Doggies: Learn How to Draw 75 Adorable Pups in All Their Glory*, *Color My Mood* with Union Square & Co., and three additional books with a local Malaysian publisher: *Bichi Mao: The Purrfect Moment*, *Bichi Mao: Our Memories*, and *Bichi Mao: Through Our Pawprints*.

I hope that this book inspires you to not only learn how to draw these adorable sea creatures, but also to create your own characters, whether they are sea life or something entirely different!

What Is Kawaii?

You might have heard the word. You have probably seen the hashtag. You definitely know the style. But what, exactly, does Kawaii mean?

Kawaii is a Japanese concept or idea, dating back to the 1970s, that translates closely to "cuteness" in English. In Japan, the usage of the word is quite broad and can be used to describe anything cute, from clothing and accessories to handwriting and art. So, if you are a fan of emoji art or the style of beloved characters like Hello Kitty, Pokémon, or Pusheen the Cat, then you already know and love the Kawaii style of art!

While there are many interpretations as to what constitutes the Kawaii art aesthetic, most people can agree that Kawaii art is usually composed of very simple black outlines, pastel colors, and characters or objects with a rounded, youthful appearance. Facial expressions in Kawaii art are minimal and characters are frequently drawn with oversized heads and smaller bodies.

How to Use This Book

After some helpful information here in the beginning of the book about tools and techniques, there are eighty step-by-step tutorials divided into five sections: Aquatic Friends, Moods, Daily Activities, Baby Swimmers, and Dressed to Impress. At the end of the book are Coloring Pages with lots of Kawaii sea creatures for you to color and decorate.

. . . .

Tools

Feel free to draw your Kawaii sea creatures with whatever you have available to you, but here are some suggestions.

TRADITIONAL TOOLS

If you're drawing your sea life with traditional tools, use a pencil, such as a 2B/HB (aka a #2 pencil) for the initial sketch, and then use a black ink pen to finish your drawing once your sketch is final. You may want to invest in a high-quality eraser to easily get rid of any unwanted lines and marks. A ruler may also be helpful for when you're working with straight lines.

For coloring your sea creatures, I recommend using colored pencils, crayons, or watercolors. Have fun experimenting with what works best for you. The coloring pages on page 142 are a great place to practice!

DIGITAL TOOLS

There are a number of software programs and apps for drawing digitally, whether you prefer drawing on a desktop, laptop, or iPad. I prefer using Procreate on an iPad, but see what works best for your artwork, equipment, and budget.

Regarding the brushes included with these programs, I like the Monoline brush in Procreate, but again, have fun experimenting.

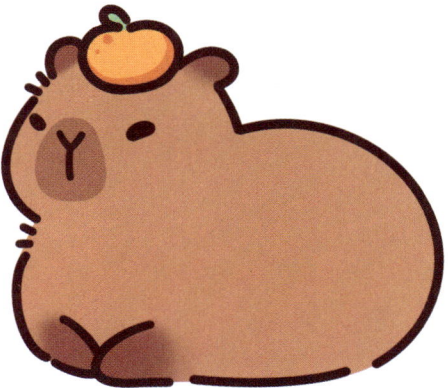

DRAWING YOUR SEA LIFE

I like to use curved lines and patterns to draw my sea creatures. That's what makes them cute and special! Here are some of the basic lines and patterns you'll see throughout the tutorials in this book.

Lines

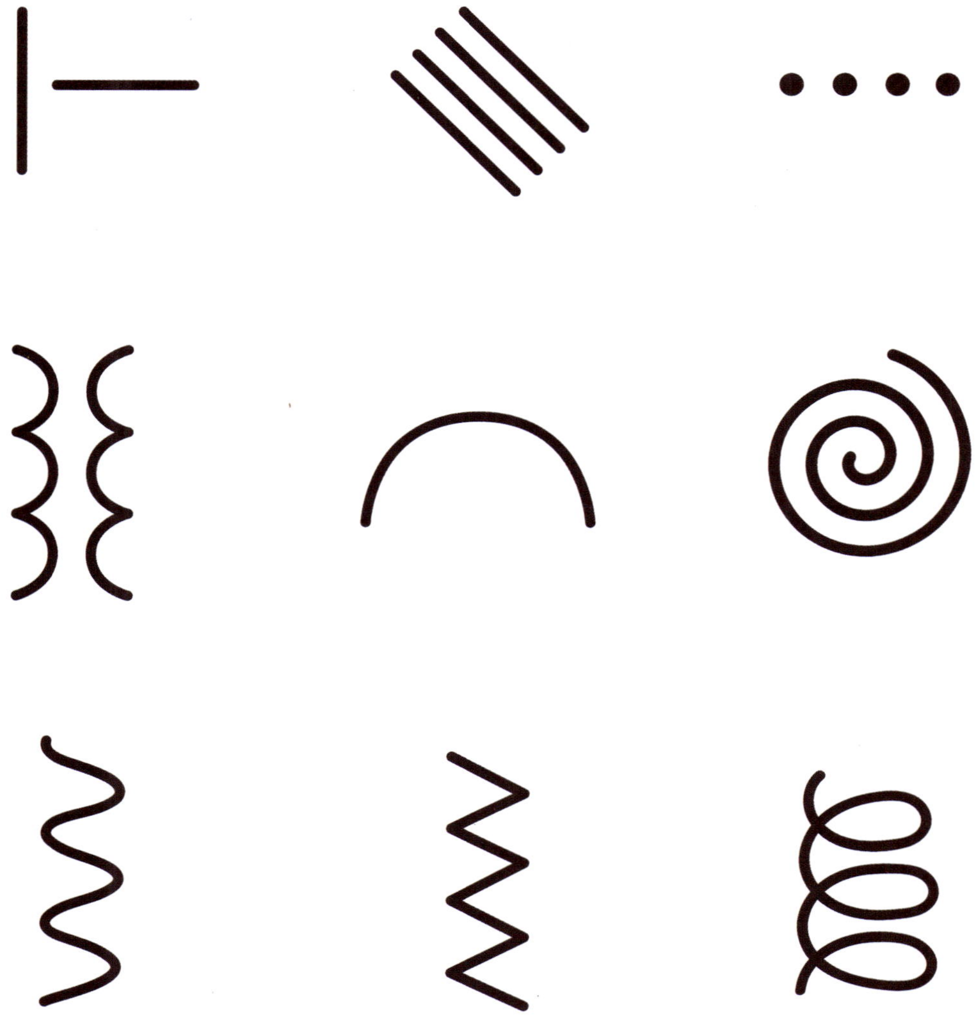

Patterns

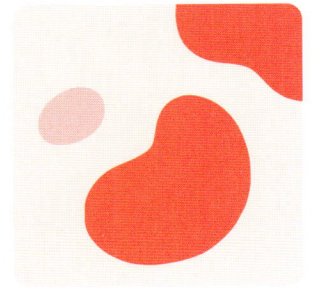

Blobs

Gradient

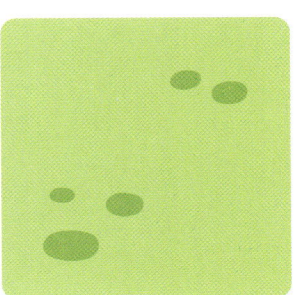

Round Spots

Oval Spots

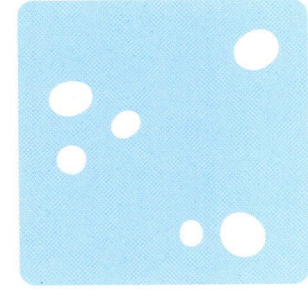

Pebbles

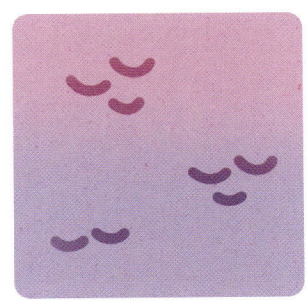

Scales

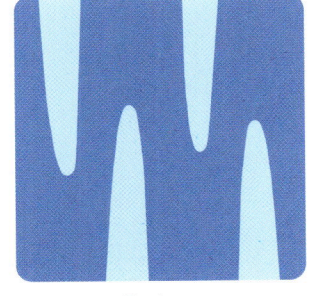

Spikes

Stripes

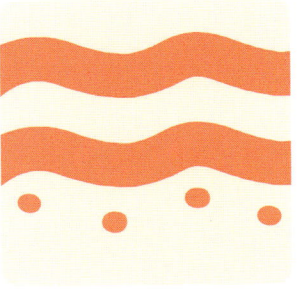

Waves

FACIAL EXPRESSION DIRECTORY

Facial expressions are what give these sea creatures their Kawaii factor. Here, I show you some of my favorite facial expressions.

Adult

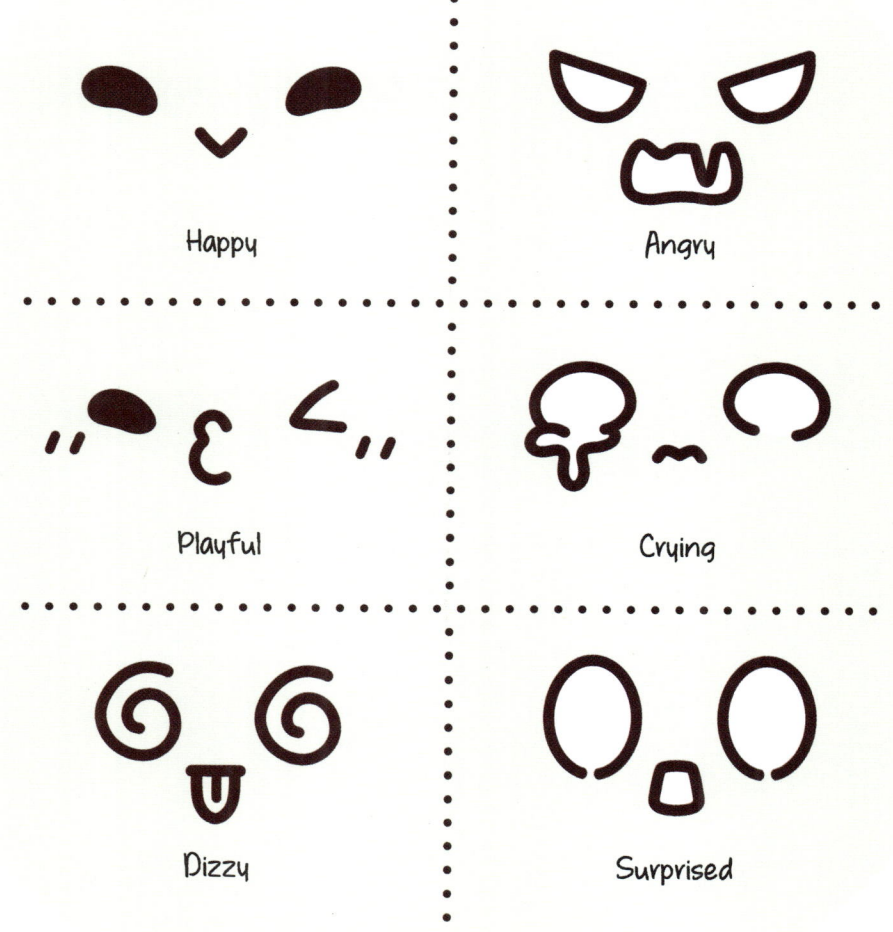

Happy

Angry

Playful

Crying

Dizzy

Surprised

Baby

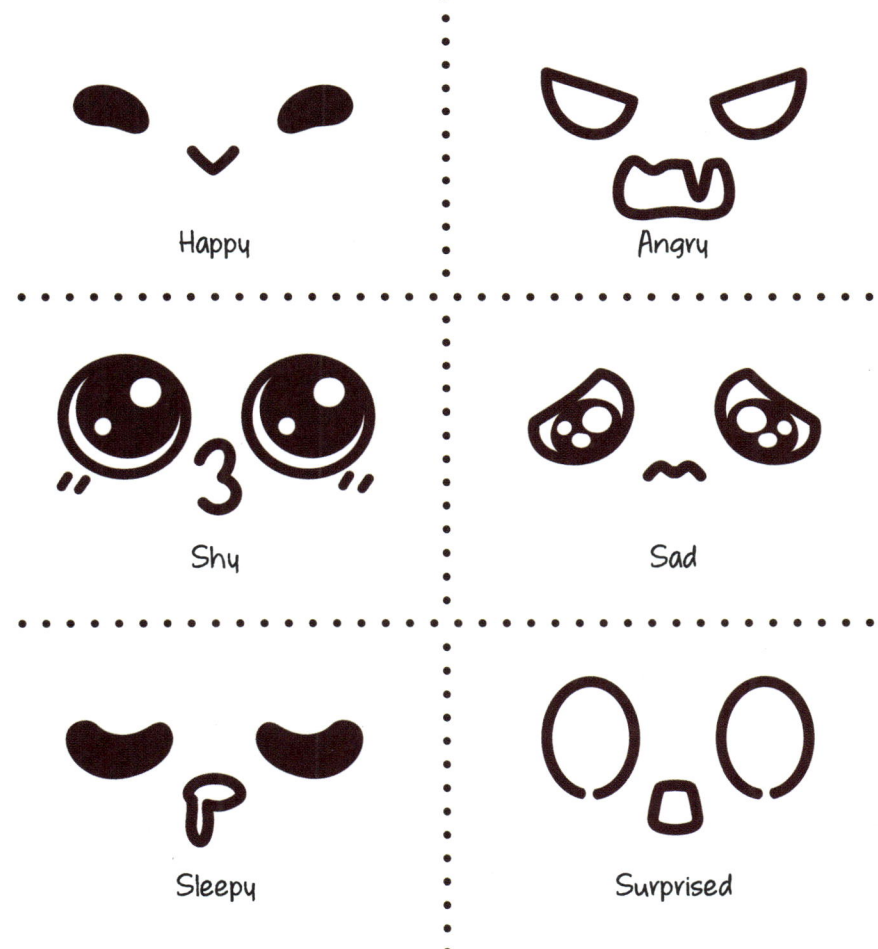

Happy

Angry

Shy

Sad

Sleepy

Surprised

COLORING YOUR SEA LIFE

I love to color my sea creatures with these colors, but your creatures can be any color you like. Who's to say a shark can't be pink? Don't forget to practice with the coloring pages on page 142!

Beige

Blue

Brown

Green

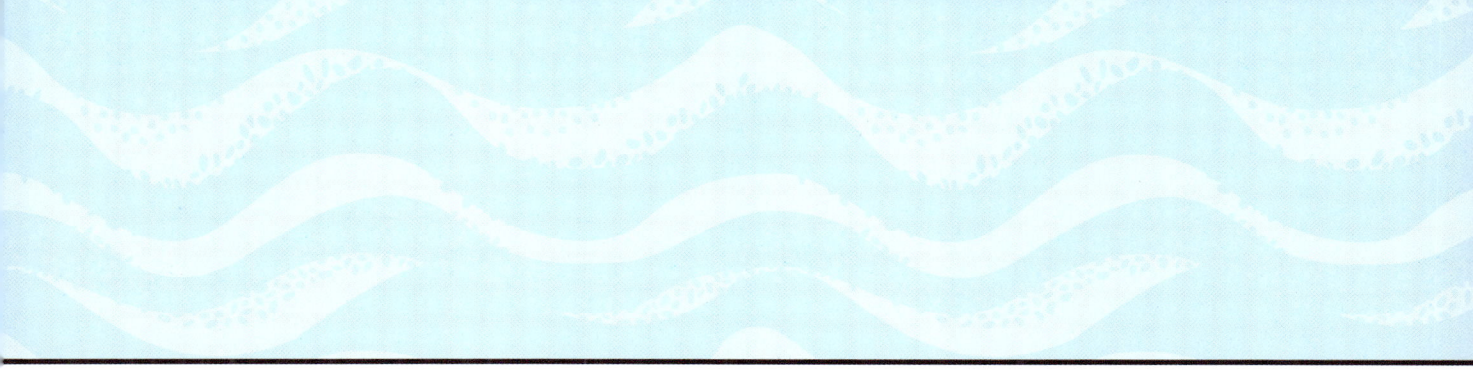

Gray

Orange

Pink

Purple

15

AQUATIC FRIENDS

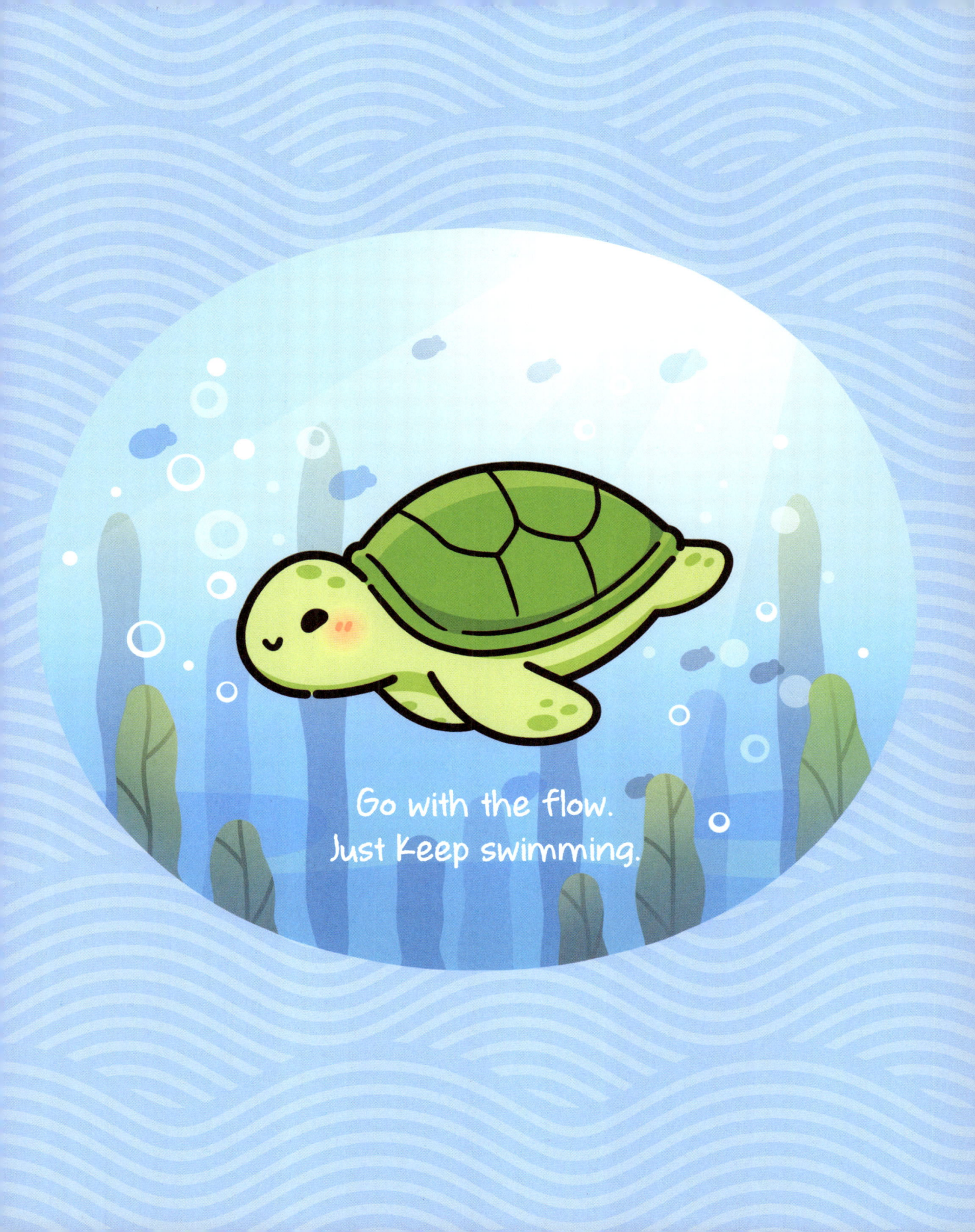

OTTER

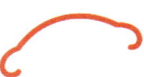

1. Draw the top of the head with ears slightly tilted.

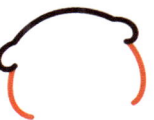

2. Draw both sides of the face with curved cheeks.

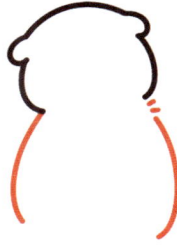

3. Draw curved lines for the sides of the body with fur detail on one side.

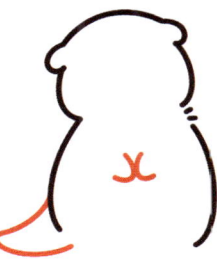

4. Add the tail as a V shape off the bottom left side of the body and little curved hands touching each other in the center of the body.

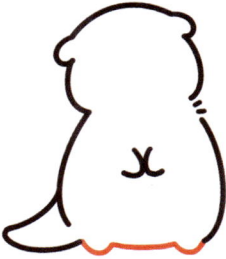

5. Complete the bottom of the body with a curved line and two stubby legs on either side.

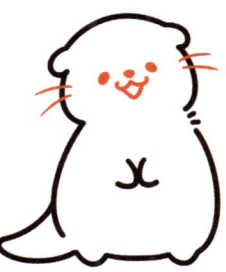

6. Finish with two whiskers on each side of the face, oval shapes for the eyes and nose, and a smiley open mouth.

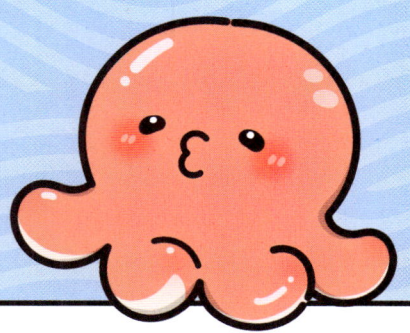

OCTOPUS

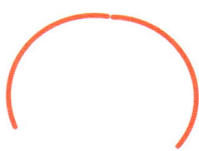

1. Draw an incomplete circle with an open bottom for the head/body.

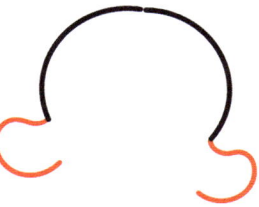

2. At the ends of the open circle, draw two tentacles extending out to the sides.

3. Add two more tentacles below the others.

4. Draw two semicircles above the middle tentacles for dimension.

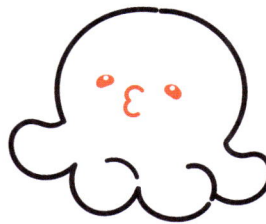

5. Finish with bean-shaped eyes and the beak as the letter E.

ANGELFISH

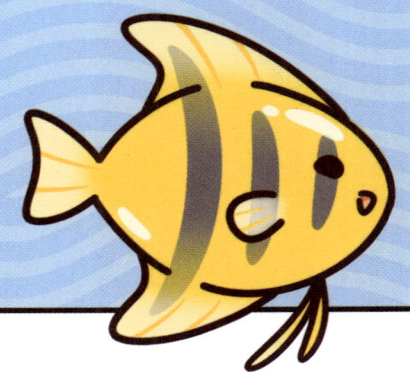

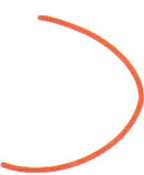

1. Draw the right side of an oval.

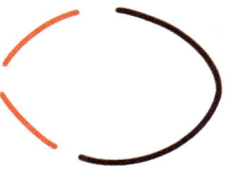

2. Draw two lines on the top and bottom of the body, disconnected from the front and angled toward each other.

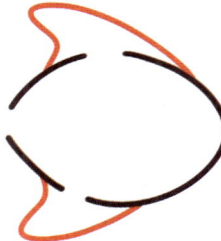

3. Draw the top and bottom fins in the shape of waves.

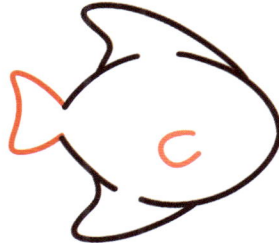

4. Add a C-shaped fin in the center of the body and a forked tail.

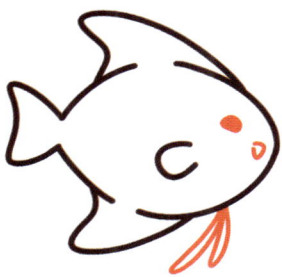

5. Finish with a bean-shaped eye, an open mouth, and two long, thin front fins below the face.

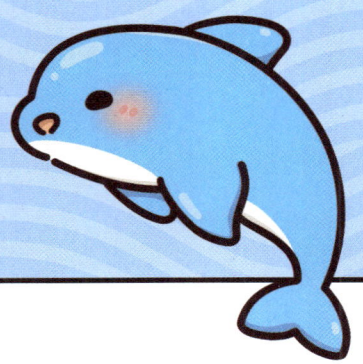

DOLPHIN

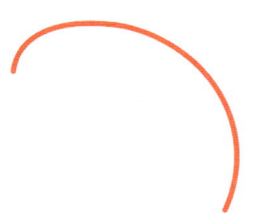

1. Start with a semicircle at an angle for the top of the head and body.

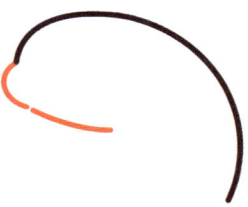

2. Draw the nose with a small, curved line and a straight line beside it.

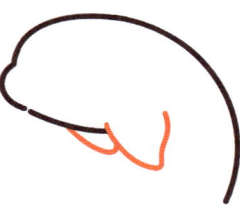

3. Add two pointed fins on the front of and behind the body.

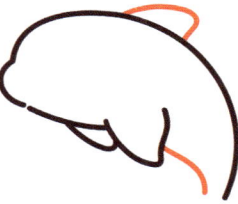

4. Add the top fin in the shape of a wave. Finish the bottom of the body with a curved line beside the front fin.

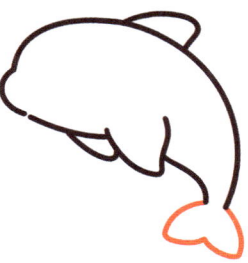

5. Draw a forked tail.

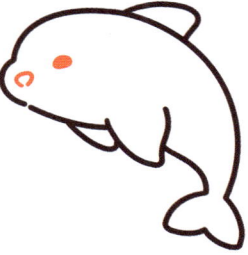

6. Finish with a bean-shaped eye and an open mouth.

SEAL

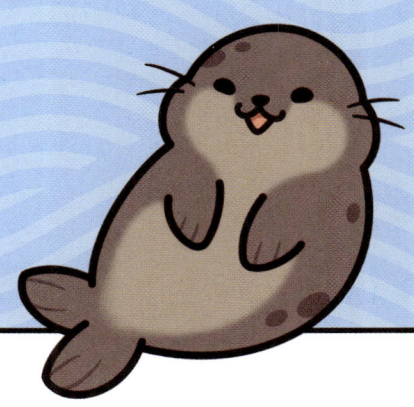

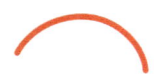

1. Draw an angled semicircle for the top of the head.

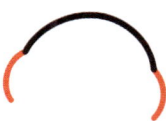

2. Add the chubby cheeks on either side of the head.

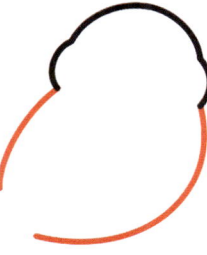

3. Draw the body of the seal with curved lines, making the right line longer for the backside.

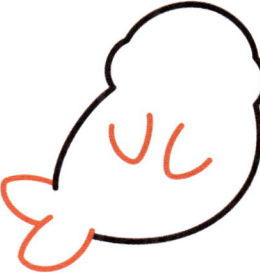

4. Draw the flippers as rounded V shapes in the center of the body. Add a forked tail at the end of the body.

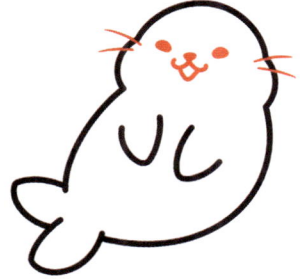

5. Finish with two whiskers on either side of the face, bean-shaped eyes, an oval nose, and a smiley open mouth.

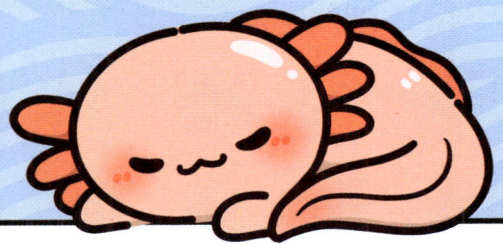

AXOLOTL

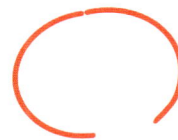

1. Draw an incomplete circle with an opening at the bottom.

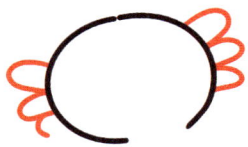

2. Draw the three external gills on either side of the circle.

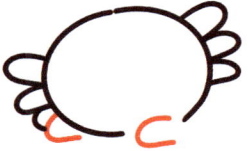

3. Use C shapes to add one arm below the left gills and the other between the circle opening.

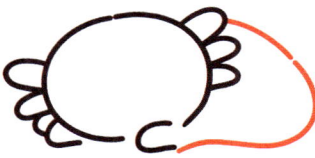

4. Draw a curved line for the body, connecting the right gills and right arm.

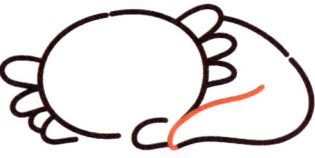

5. Draw a curved line to make the tail.

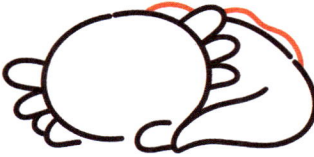

6. Add a wavy fin to the top ridge of the body.

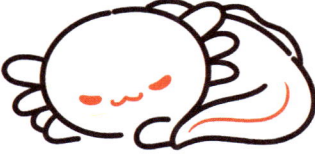

7. Finish with a curved line in the center of the tail, bean-shaped eyes, and a mouth as a sideways E.

ANGLERFISH

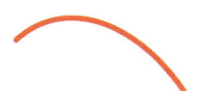

1. Draw a curved line.

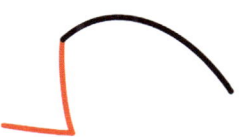

2. Connect a V shape to the line for the mouth.

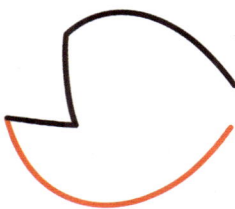

3. Add a curved line below for the bottom of the head/body.

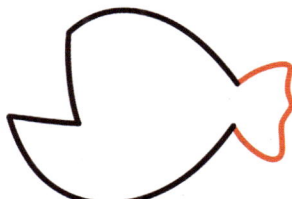

4. Draw a tail with three points.

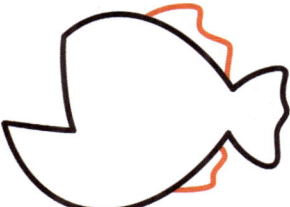

5. Draw fins on the top and bottom of the head/body in the shape of waves.

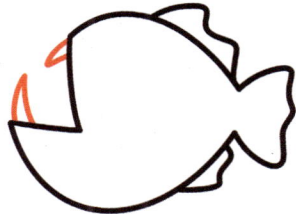

6. Draw a small tooth on the top of the mouth and a bigger tooth on the bottom, both pointed and on the edge of the mouth.

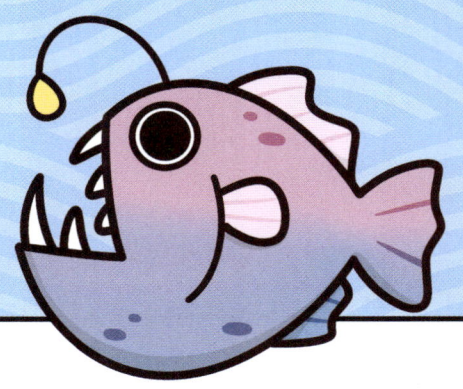

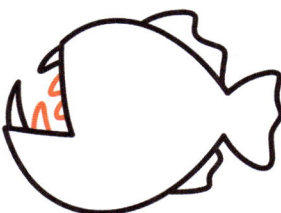

7. Add more pointed teeth inside the mouth, varying in size.

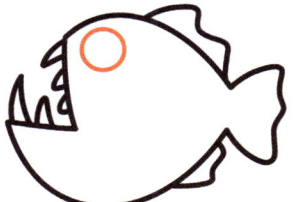

8. Draw a circle near the top of the head/body for an eye.

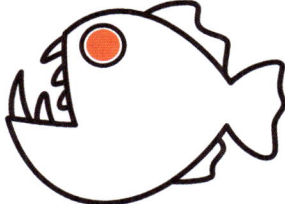

9. Almost completely fill in the eye for the pupil.

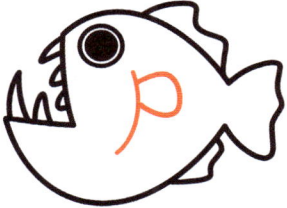

10. Add a curved line in the center of the body for a gill and a backward C for a fin.

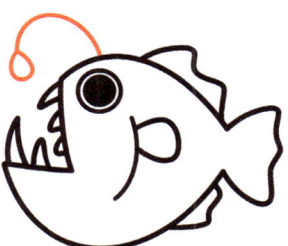

11. Draw the lure of the fish with a curved line off the top of the head, ending with a small circle for the light.

NARWHAL

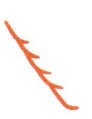

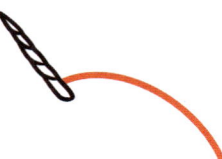

1. Draw a slanted line with small lines attached like thorns.

2. Draw a line on the other side of the thorns to create the horn.

3. Draw a curved line on the bottom right side of the horn.

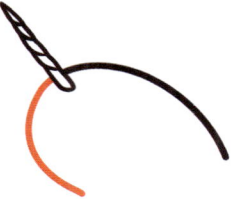

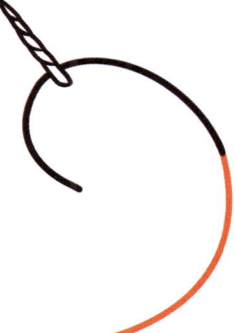

4. Draw a shorter, more curved line on the bottom left side of the horn for the face.

5. Draw the curved line of the bottom right side of the body.

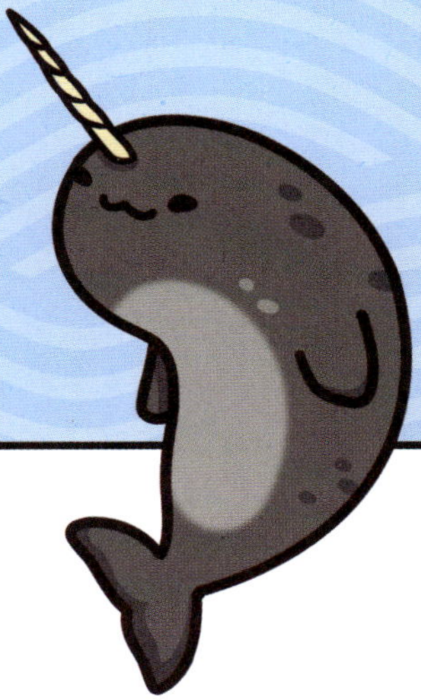

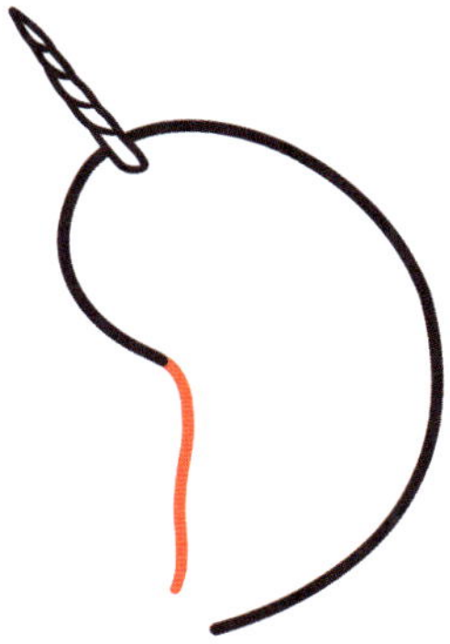

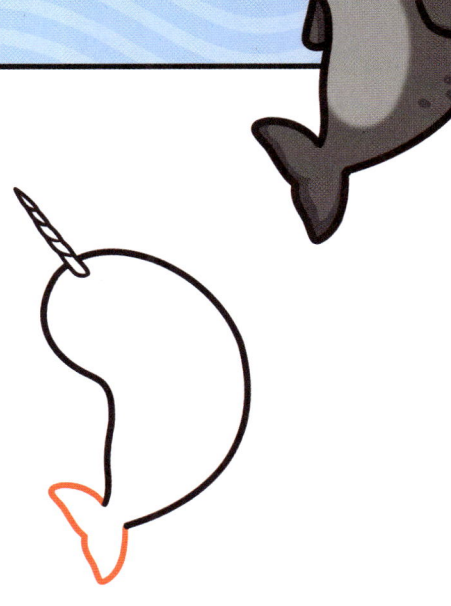

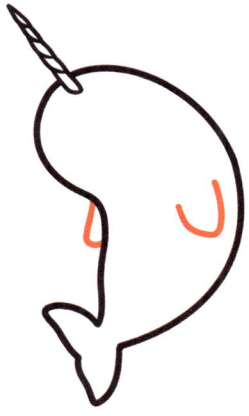

6. Draw a slightly squiggly line extending below the face.

7. Add a forked tail at the end of the body.

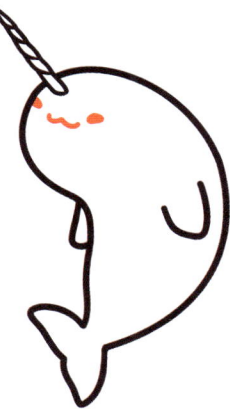

8. Draw U-shaped fins in the middle of the body and below the face.

9. Finish with bean-shaped eyes and a sideways-E mouth.

CROCODILE

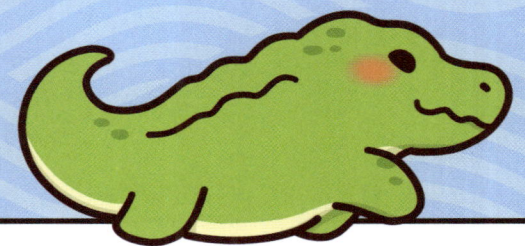

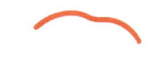

1. Draw a line with two ridges.

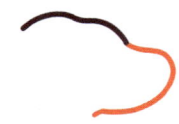

2. Add the snout on the right side with an upturned nose.

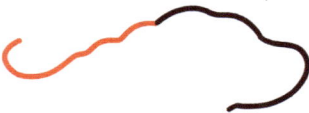

3. Draw a ridged line extending from the top of the head that ends in a curl.

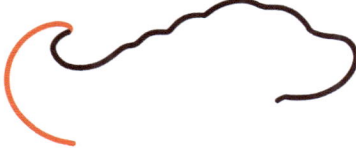

4. Draw a curved line from the curl to the bottom of the body for the tail.

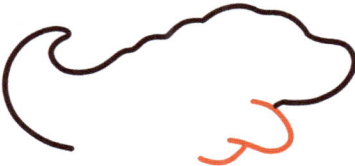

5. Draw the front arm as a backward C below the snout and the back arm as a curved line beside the front arm.

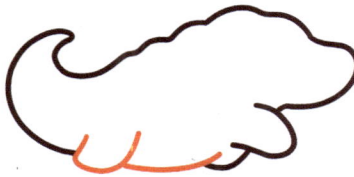

6. Draw the curved line of the stomach. Add a U-shaped leg between the tail and stomach.

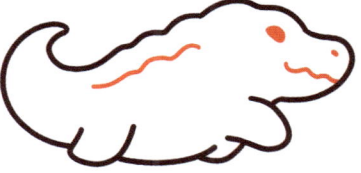

7. Finish with a bean-shaped eye, a dot for a nose on the end of the snout, and a squiggly line for the sharp-toothed mouth. Add a squiggly line below the top of the body for dimension.

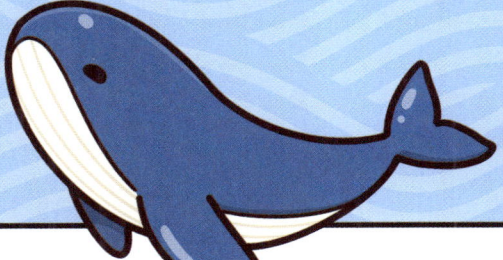

BLUE WHALE

1. Start with a curved line for the top of the head.

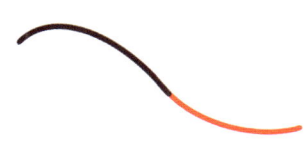

2. Draw and connect another curved line.

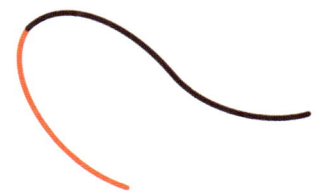

3. Draw the curved line of the mouth.

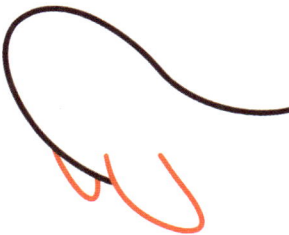

4. Draw paddle-shaped fins on the front and back of the body, below the mouth.

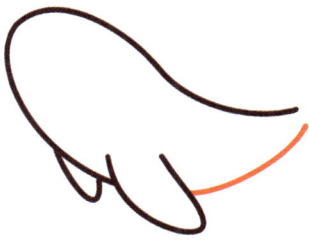

5. Finish the body by drawing a curved line from the front fin to the top of the body.

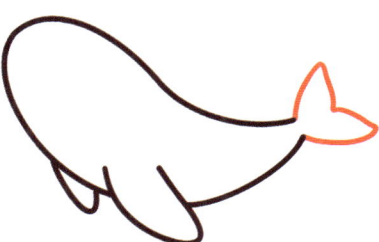

6. Add a forked tail.

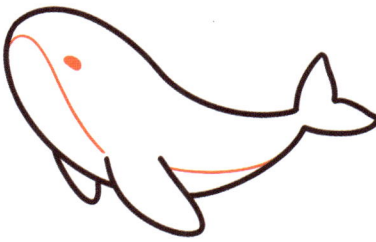

7. Finish with a bean-shaped eye and a curved line for the mouth, extending just beyond the front fin.

CAPYBARA

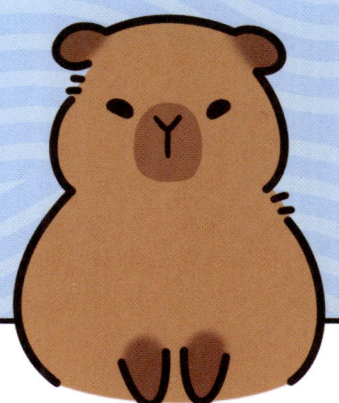

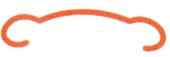

1. Draw the ears and a curved line to connect them.

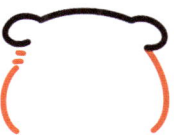

2. Draw the curved cheeks on either side of the head with fur texture below one ear.

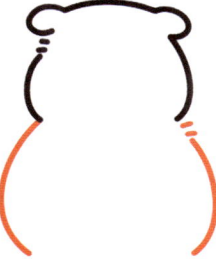

3. Draw the curved body on either side with fur texture below one cheek.

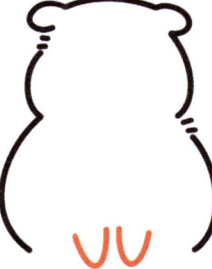

4. Add two V-shaped paws at the bottom of the body.

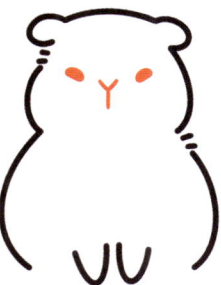

5. Finish with bean-shaped eyes and a Y-shaped mouth.

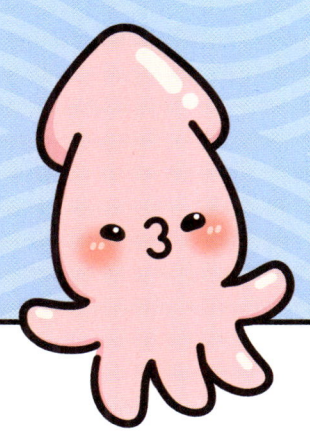

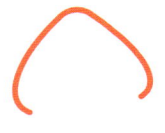

1. Start with a semicircle for the head with an almost-point at the top.

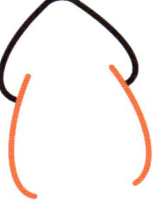

2. Add two curved lines for either side of the face.

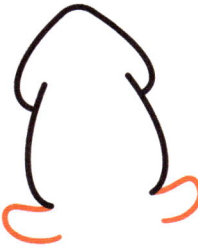

3. Draw two tentacles extending out to the sides.

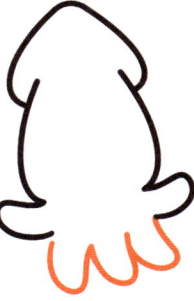

4. Add three tentacles at the bottom of the body.

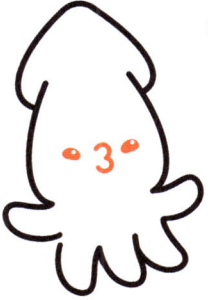

5. Finish with bean-shaped eyes, leaving a little white for the pupils, and a beak like the number three.

PENGUIN

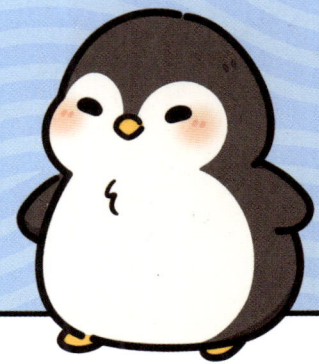

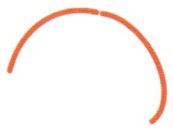

1. Start with a semicircle at an angle.

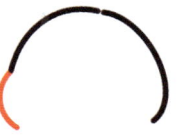

2. Draw a curved line for a chubby cheek.

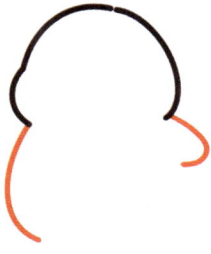

3. Draw a longer, curved line below the cheek for the body. Add a flipper on the right side.

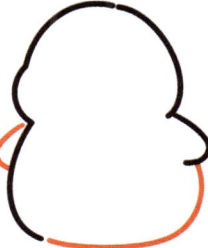

4. Draw another flipper below the cheek and behind the body. Connect the stomach to the front flipper with a curved line.

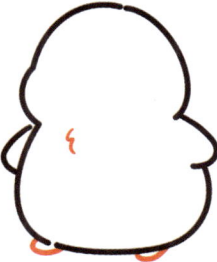

5. Add two feet. Draw fur texture on the chest in the shape of a wave.

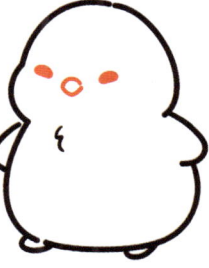

6. Finish with bean-shaped eyes and a triangle-shaped beak.

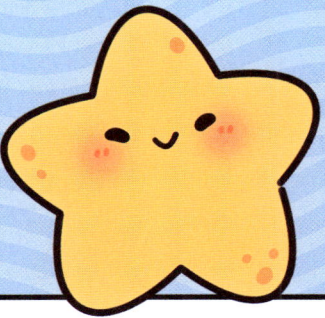

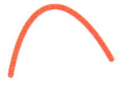

1. Draw the top half of an oval for the top of the head/body.

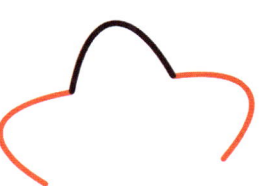

2. Draw the same shape for the arms on both sides.

3. Draw the same shape for the legs to complete the five-point shape.

4. Finish with bean-shaped eyes and a small smile.

JELLYFISH

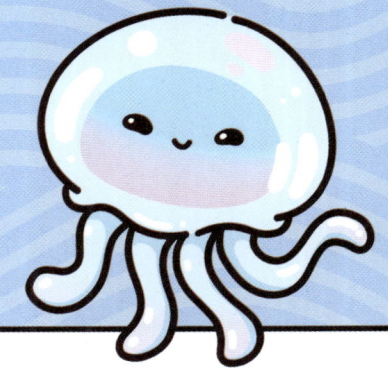

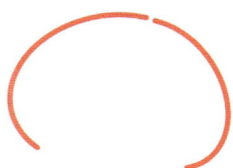

1. Draw an incomplete circle.

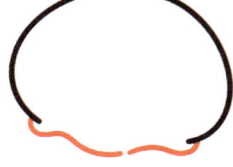

2. Draw a wavy line to finish the circle.

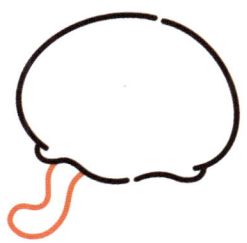

3. Draw one tentacle on the left at a curve.

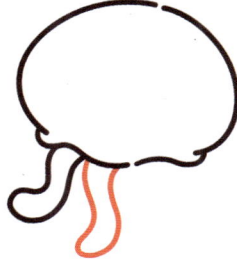

4. Add another tentacle beside it curving in the same direction.

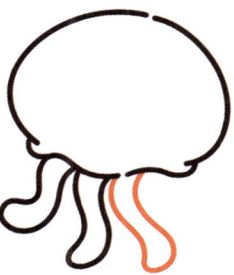

5. Add another, longer tentacle curving in the same direction.

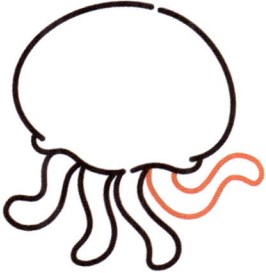

6. Add the last curved tentacle drawn in the opposite direction.

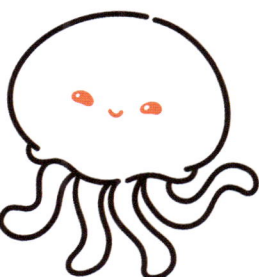

7. Finish with bean-shaped eyes, leaving a little white for the pupils, and a small smile.

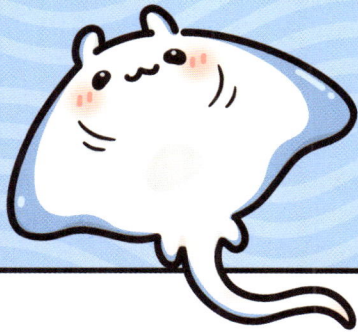

MANTA RAY

1. Draw the front of the head with two ears and a curved line in between.

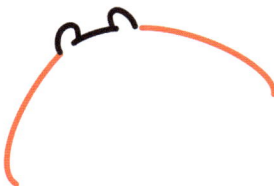

2. Draw the top of the fins with a curved line on each side.

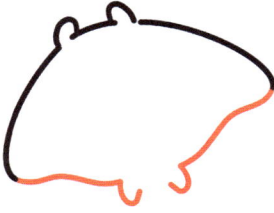

3. Draw the bottom of the body with slightly wavy lines leading into the pelvic fins.

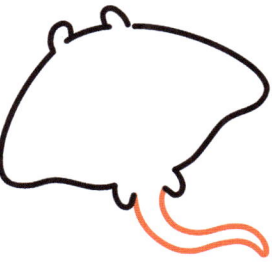

4. Add the tail with a curve at the end for movement.

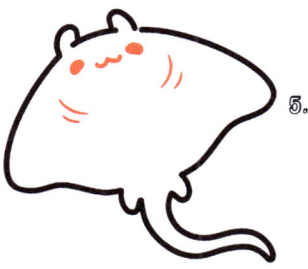

5. Finish with bean-shaped eyes, a sideways-E mouth, and four curved lines for gills below the face.

LOBSTER

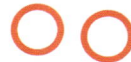

1. Draw two circles side by side for the eyes.

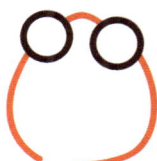

2. Draw a curved line between the eyes with an almost-point at the top and curved lines for the cheeks.

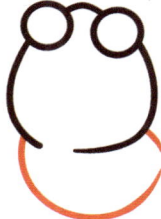

3. Draw a circle below and slightly covered by the head.

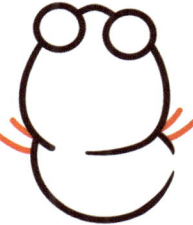

4. Add two arms at the top of the body with two parallel lines extending up.

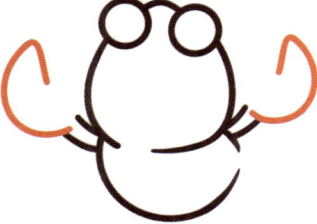

5. Draw two almost complete half circles at the ends of the arms.

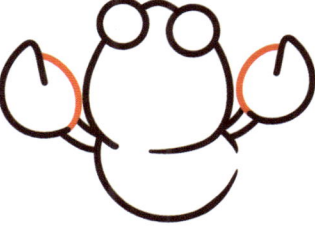

6. Draw curved lines from the arms almost to the ends of the half circles to finish the claws.

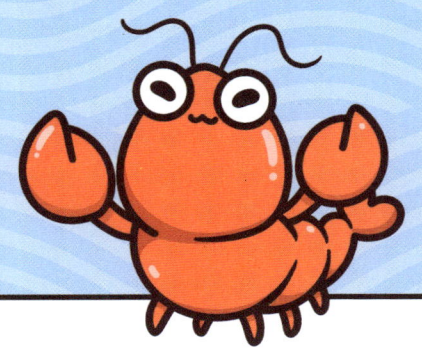

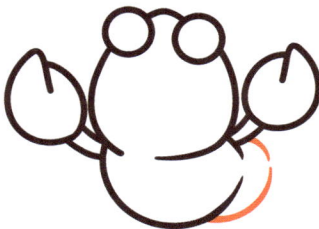

7. Draw two curved lines that almost meet behind the body to continue the abdomen.

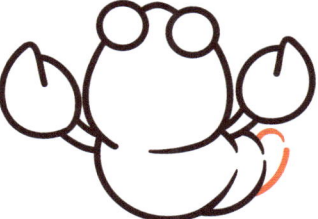

8. Draw another two, smaller curved lines that almost meet.

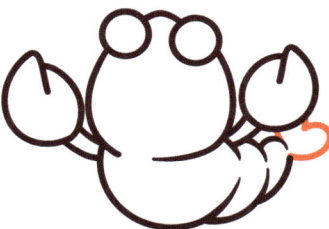

9. Draw a forked tail at the end of the body, hidden by the claw.

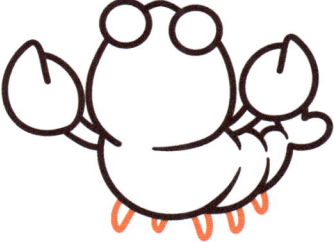

10. Add five legs below the body, with bigger ones in front and smaller behind.

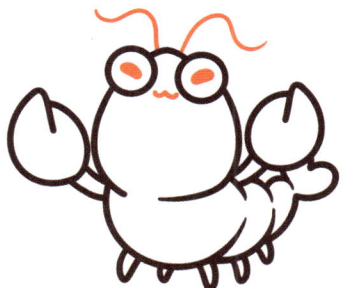

11. Finish with bean-shaped pupils in the eyes, a sideways-E mouth, and two curvy antennae.

SEAHORSE

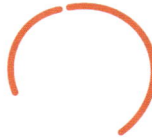

1. Draw an incomplete circle.

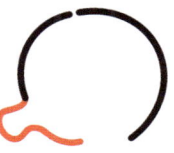

2. Draw the long snout and the bottom of the face with a curved line.

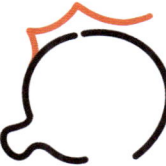

3. Draw the fin with two waves on top of the head.

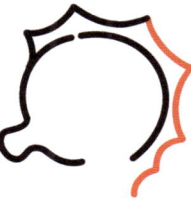

4. Add four more fin waves on the back of the head.

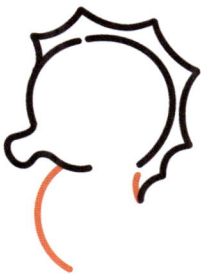

5. Draw the longer, curved line of the stomach below the snout and a smaller, curved line connecting the back of the head to the fin.

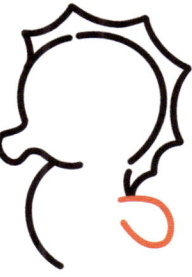

6. Draw an arm fin below the head extending from the body.

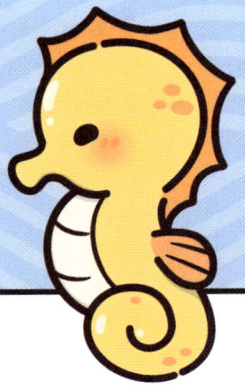

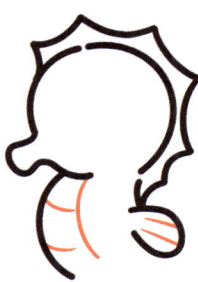

7. Add details such as lines on the arm fin and the lines of the chest.

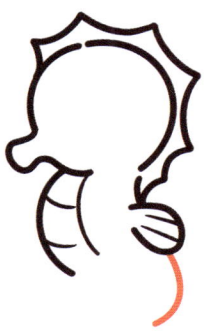

8. Draw a curved line below the fin.

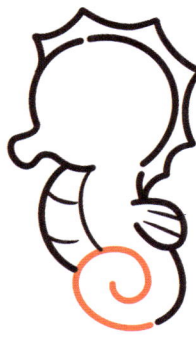

9. Draw a a swirl below the stomach, connecting to the bottom of the body.

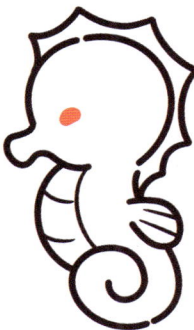

10. Finish with a bean-shaped eye.

WALRUS

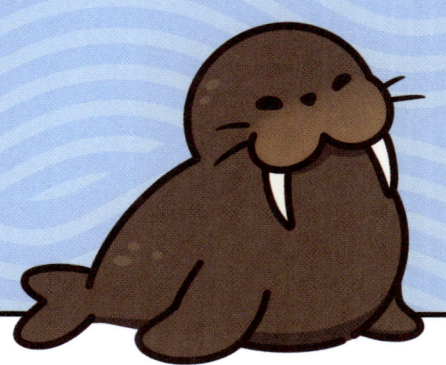

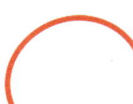

1. Draw a semicircle at an angle.

2. Add a sideways three connecting to one side of the head.

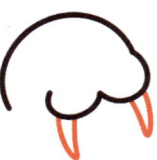

3. Draw two tusks coming out of the E curves.

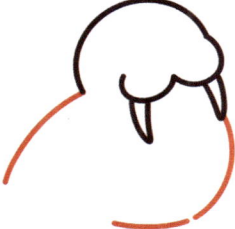

4. Draw a curved line extending from the head and a half circle from the right tusk.

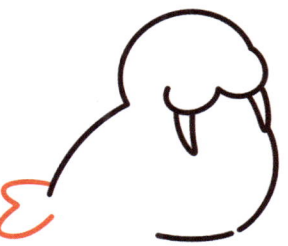

5. Draw a forked tail at the end of the body.

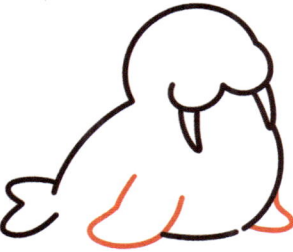

6. Add a paddle-like flipper on the front of the body and a smaller flipper behind the body.

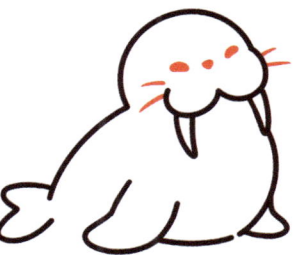

7. Finish with bean-shaped eyes, a triangular nose, and whiskers on either side of the face.

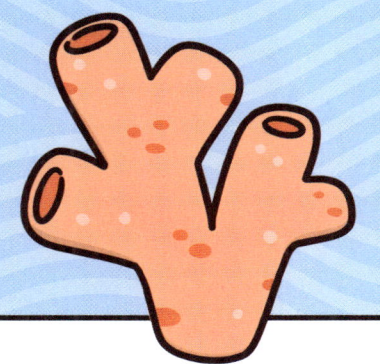

CORAL

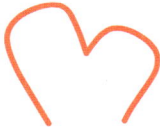

1. Draw a heart shape with an open bottom.

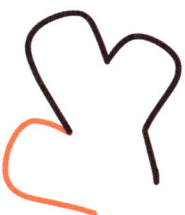

2. Add a C-shaped line on one side and a short straight line on the other.

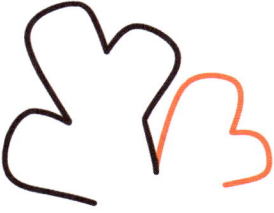

3. Draw another open-bottomed heart shape connected to the short, straight line.

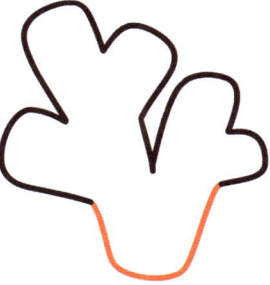

4. Complete the shape with a U-like, curved line.

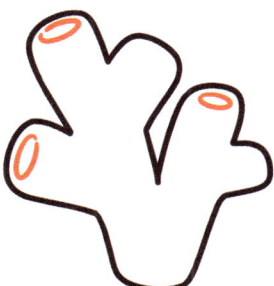

5. Finish with ovals near the tops of three of the coral arms.

SEA TURTLE

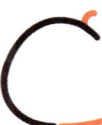

1. Draw a C shape at an angle for the head.

2. Draw a line below for the neck and a small, curved line above for the shell ridge.

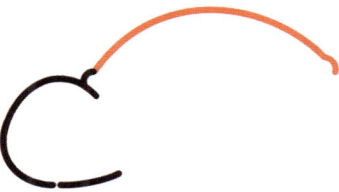

3. Draw a curved line for the top of the shell, ending with a smaller, curved line for the shell ridge.

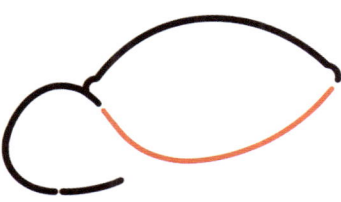

4. Add a curved line for the bottom of the shell.

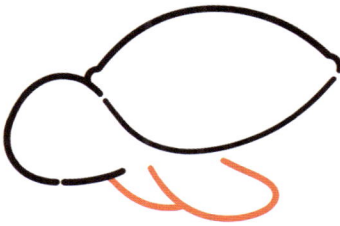

5. Draw the paddle-like flippers below the shell, with the back one as a curved line connecting the head and the front flipper.

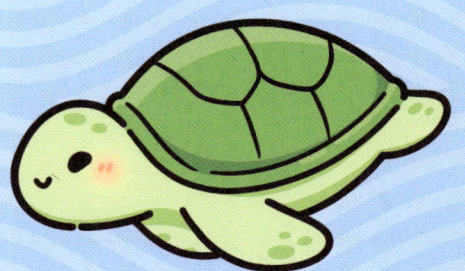

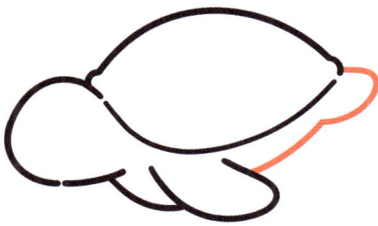

6. Draw a line parallel to the shell and then draw the back leg that connects to the shell.

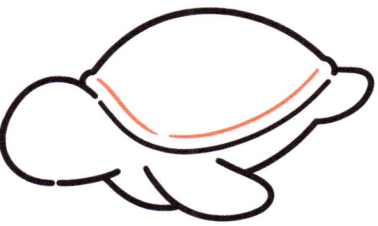

7. Add a line along the shell's edge to form the ridge.

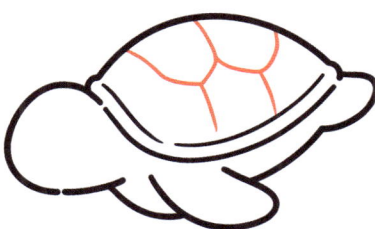

8. Draw the hexagonal shapes on the turtle's shell.

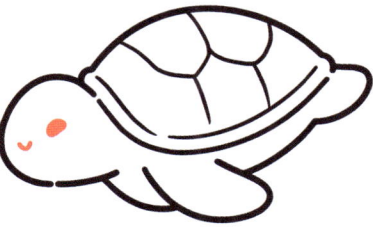

9. Finish with a bean-shaped eye and a small smile.

SHARK

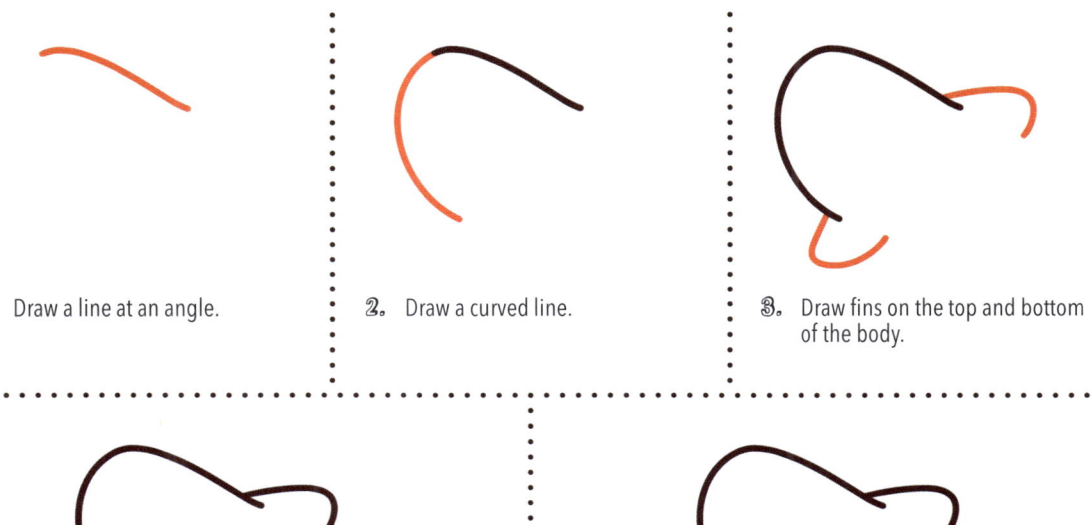

1. Draw a line at an angle.

2. Draw a curved line.

3. Draw fins on the top and bottom of the body.

4. Draw two short lines to the right of the fins.

5. Draw another larger, paddle-like fin starting from the center of the body.

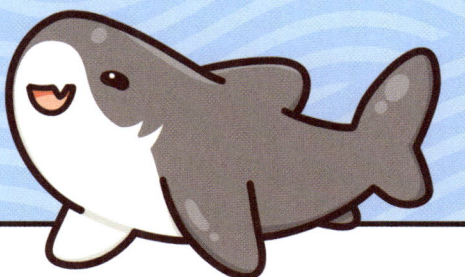

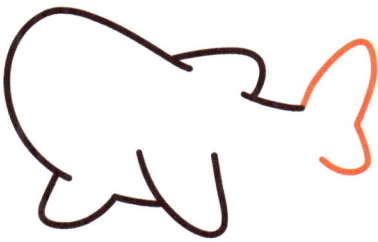

6. Add a tail at the end of the body in the shape of an ear.

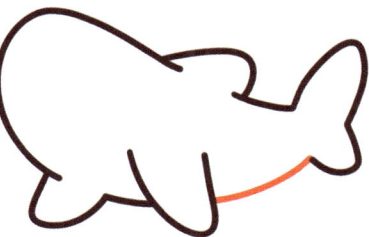

7. Draw a curved line to connect the front fin and the tail.

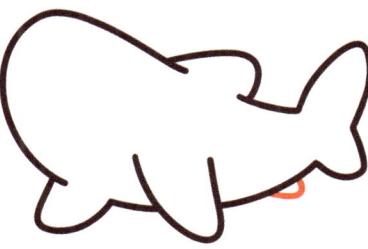

8. Between the front fin and tail, add a small fin.

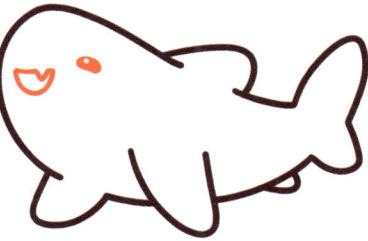

9. Finish with a bean-shaped eye, leaving a little white for the pupil, and an open-mouthed smile with a sharp tooth.

CLAM

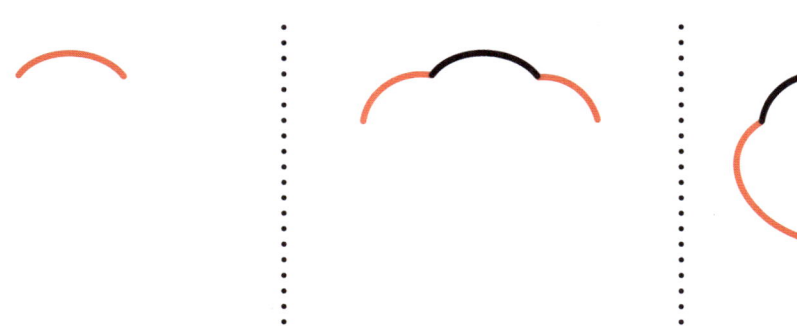

1. Draw a curved line.

2. Draw two identically sized curved lines on each side at an angle.

3. Draw two curved lines below to create an oval shape with an open bottom.

4. Draw curved lines extending out and below the oval.

5. Draw a series of curved lines in five waves to reflect the curves at the top of the shape.

6. Connect the ends of the bottom oval shape in one curved line.

7. Add two curved lines like two hills inside the bottom shell.

8. Draw an open-bottomed circle at the bottom of the top shell.

9. Finish with bean-shaped eyes and a sideways-E mouth inside the bottom shell.

CLOWNFISH

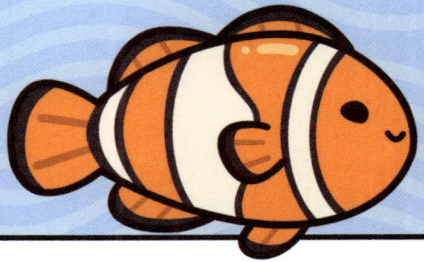

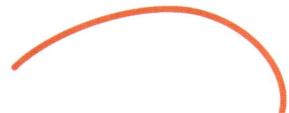

1. Draw a curved line for the top of the head/body.

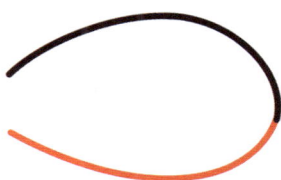

2. Draw an identical but mirrored curved line for the bottom of the head/body.

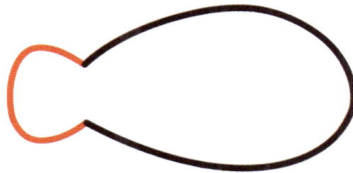

3. Draw a C-shaped tail at the end of the head/body.

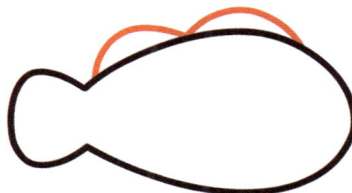

4. Add the fins to the top of the head/body with two curved lines in a row.

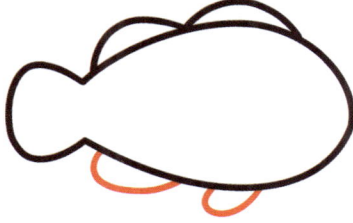

5. Add two fins below the body, with a small fin in the front and a longer fin in the back.

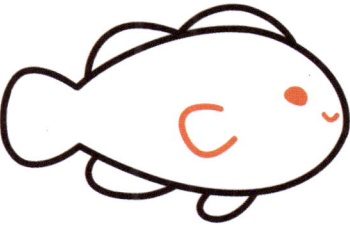

6. Finish with a C-shaped fin, a bean-shaped eye, and a small smile.

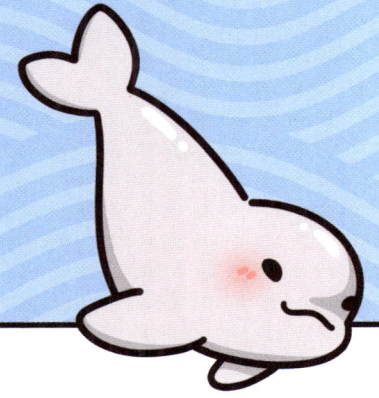

BELUGA WHALE

1. Draw a curved line at an angle.

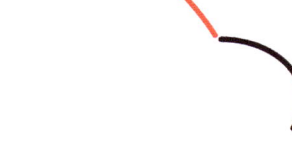

2. Connect a straight line at an angle off the curved line.

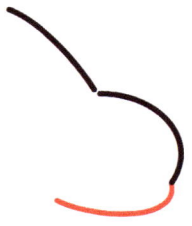

3. Draw a curved line at the bottom to finish the head.

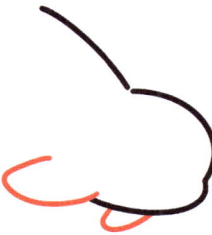

4. Draw the paddle-like fins in front and behind the body.

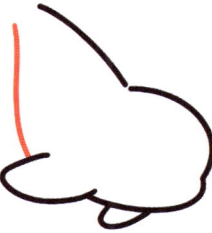

5. Draw a curved line heading toward the top of the body.

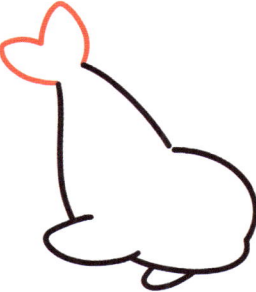

6. Add a forked tail.

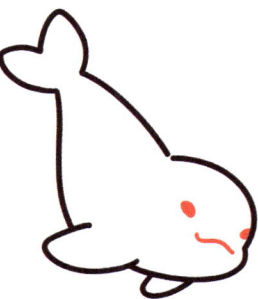

7. Finish with bean-shaped eyes and a curvy mouth.

ORCA

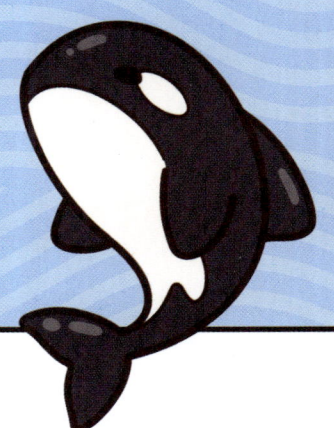

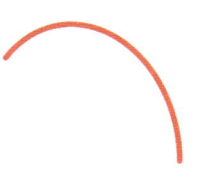

1. Draw a curved line for the top of the head/body.

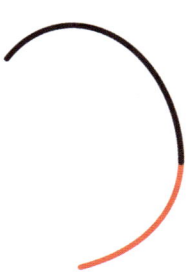

2. Continue the curved line downward and toward the tail.

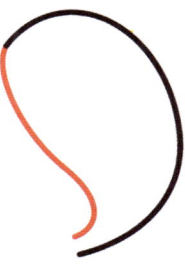

3. Draw an almost S-shaped curve from the face leading toward the tail.

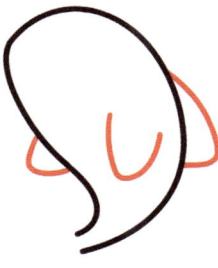

4. Add the fins. Draw C-shaped fins on the left side of the body and in the center of the body, and a larger fin on the top of the body.

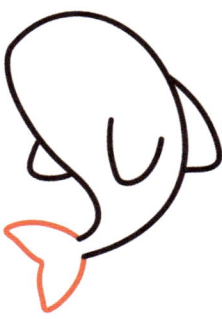

5. Draw a tail with flukes at the end of the body.

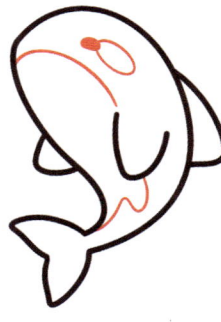

6. Finish with a bean-shaped eye with an open oval next to it, a curved line for the mouth and markings, and jagged lines for more markings near the fin.

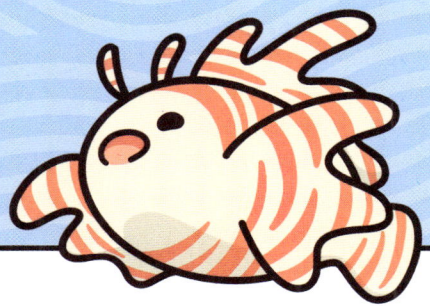

LIONFISH

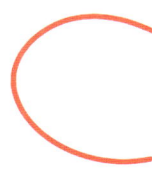

1. Draw the left two-thirds of an oval for the head/body.

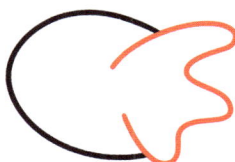

2. Draw a winglike fin from the center of the head/body with three curved peaks.

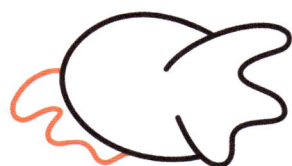

3. Draw another winglike fin beside the left of the head with three curved peaks.

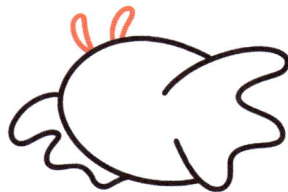

4. Draw two rounded spines on top of the head.

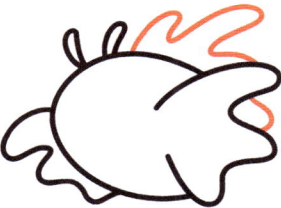

5. Add another winglike fin on top of the body with four curved peaks.

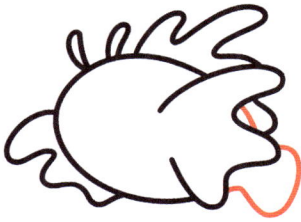

6. Draw a C-shaped tail at the end of the head/body.

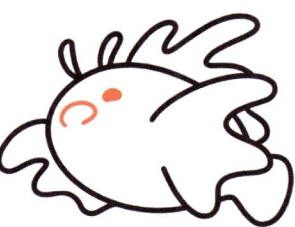

7. Finish with a bean-shaped eye and an open-circle mouth.

SWORDFISH

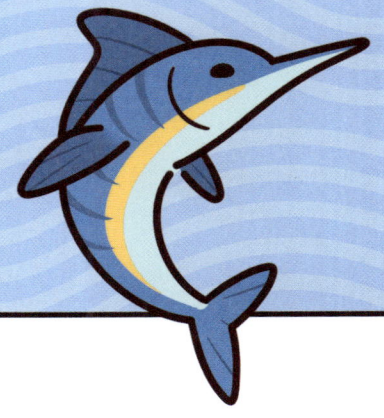

1. Draw a curved line for the top of the head.

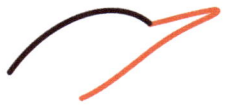

2. Draw the pointed mouth and the bottom of the head.

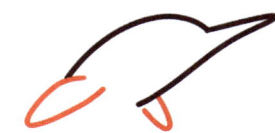

3. Draw two paddle-like fins on either side of the body.

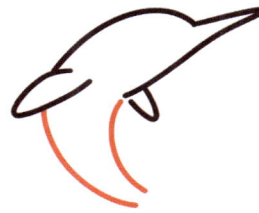

4. Draw two curved lines next to each other and angled so the body forms a C shape.

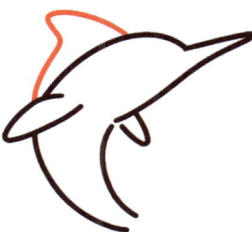

5. Add a fin on top of the head in a wave shape.

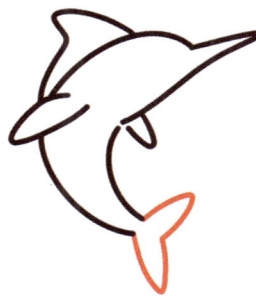

6. Draw a forked tail at the end of the body.

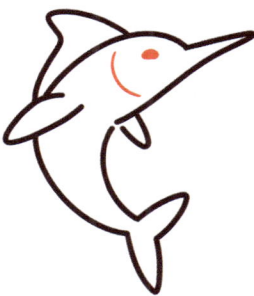

7. Finish with a bean-shaped eye and a curved line next to the face for gills.

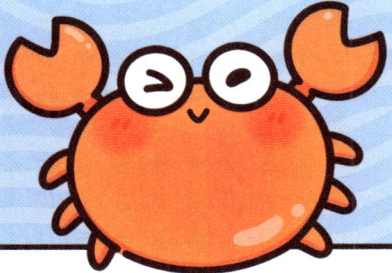

CRAB

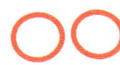

1. Draw two circles side by side for the eyes.

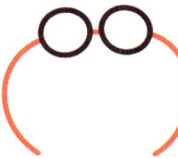

2. Draw a line between the circles and two half circles to make the body.

3. Finish the circle at the bottom of the body. Draw two parallel lines on each side of the eyes for the arms.

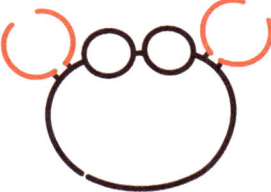

4. Draw two incomplete circles at the ends of the arms.

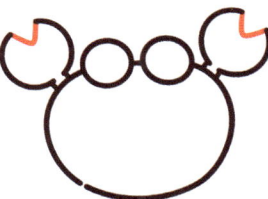

5. Add a V to the incomplete circles to finish the claws.

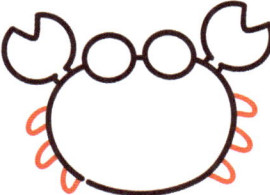

6. Add three legs on each side of the body.

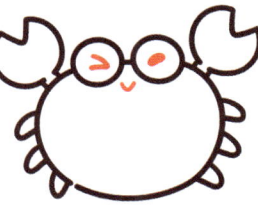

7. Finish with a V-shaped smile, a bean-shaped eye, and a winking eye using a sideways V.

ELECTRIC EEL

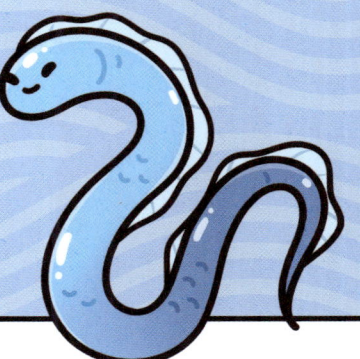

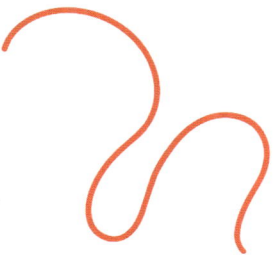

1. Draw a curvy line with two high peaks, like a camel's back.

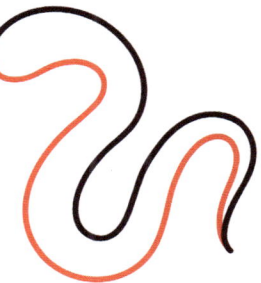

2. Draw another curvy line parallel to the first one with a rounded head and pointed tail.

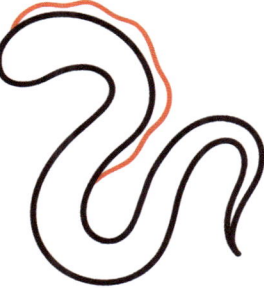

3. Add a wavy-lined fin from the top of the head to just before the middle of the body.

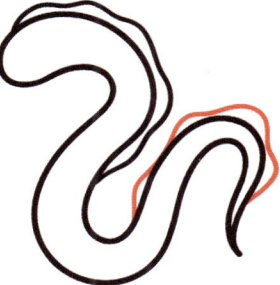

4. Add another wavy-lined fin from just after the middle of the body to the tail.

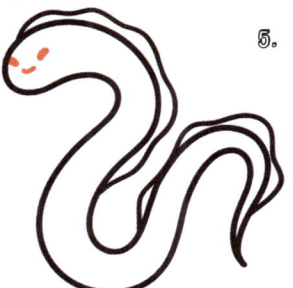

5. Finish with bean-shaped eyes and a small smile.

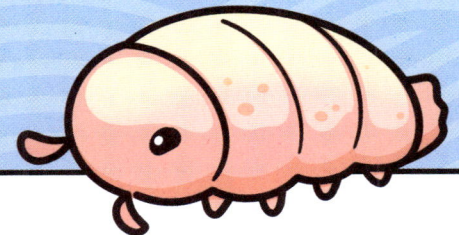

ISOPOD

1. Draw a semicircle.

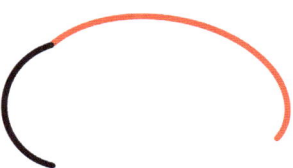

2. Draw a longer, horizontal curved line.

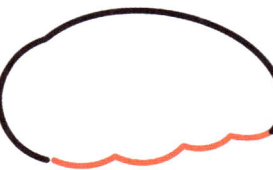

3. Draw four curved lines in a row to close the shape.

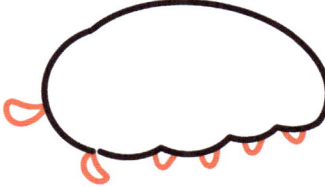

4. Add two antennae on the head and four small legs along the body.

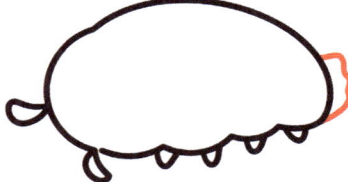

5. Draw a tail like a webbed foot.

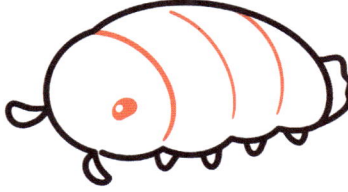

6. Finish with a bean-shaped eye, leaving a little white for the pupil, and three curved lines for each ridge of the body.

MOODS

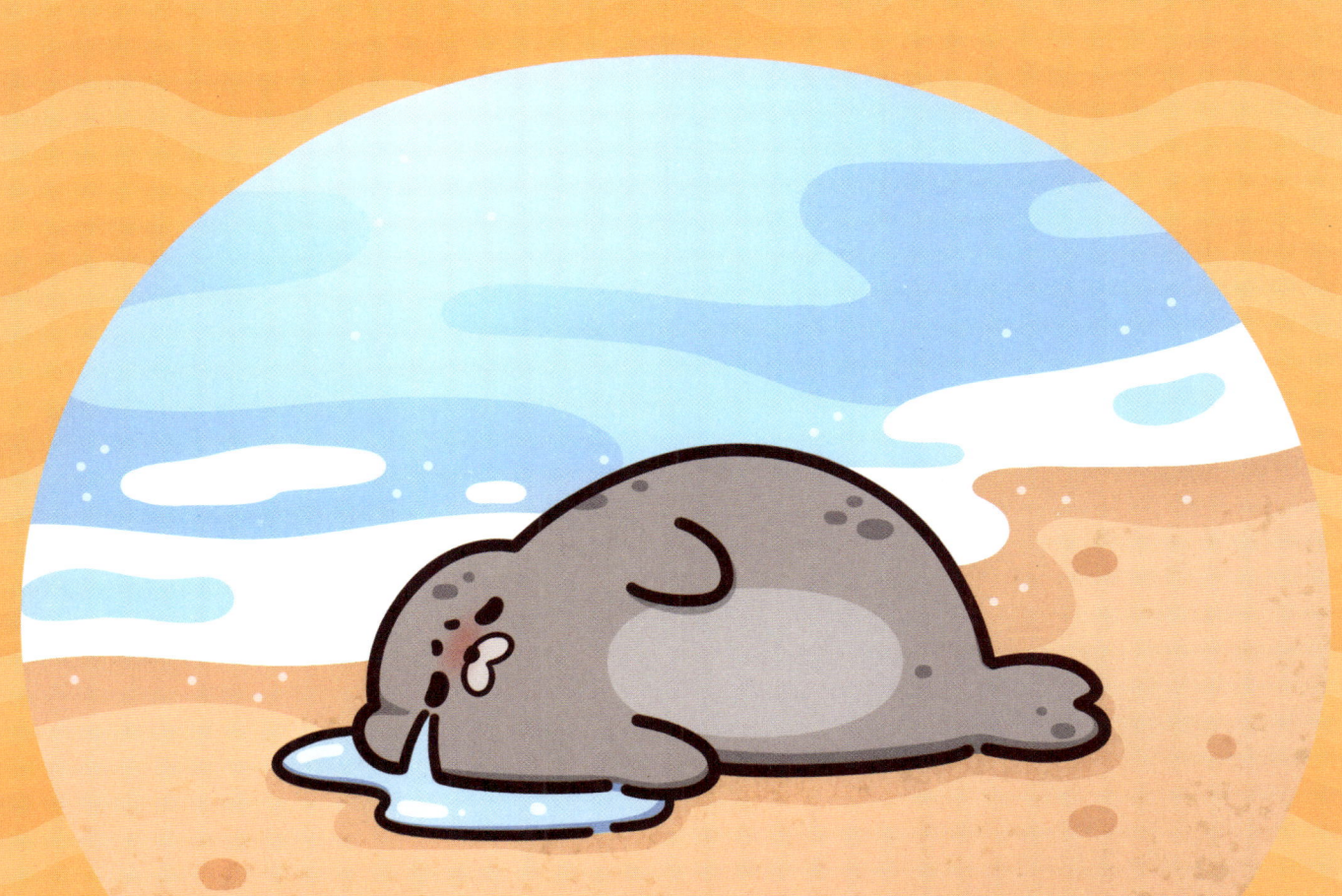

BRB, don't mind me.
I'm in my sad seal era.

JOYFUL DOLPHIN

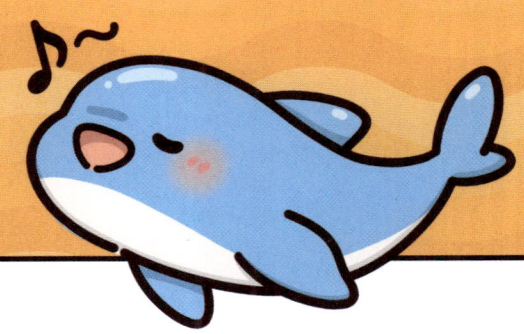

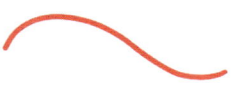

1. Draw a curvy line.

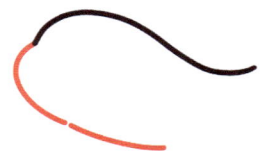

2. Draw a curved line to create the nose and connect a straight line for the bottom of the body.

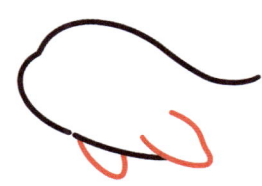

3. Add two paddle-like fins below the face and from the center of the body.

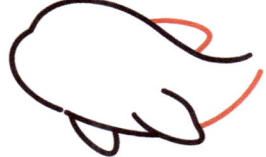

4. Draw a curved line from the front fin in the direction of the top of the body. Add the top fin in the shape of a wave.

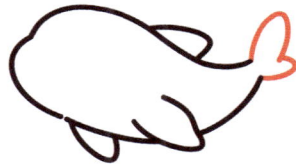

5. Add a forked tail in the shape of a mitten.

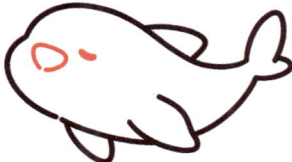

6. Draw a bean-shaped closed eye and an open mouth.

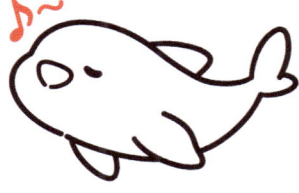

7. Finish with a musical note and a squiggly line above the head.

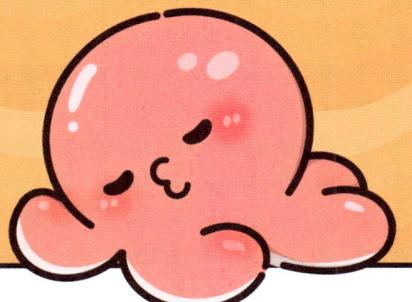

SLEEPY OCTOPUS

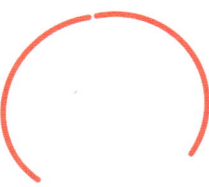

1. Draw an incomplete circle with an open bottom for the head/body.

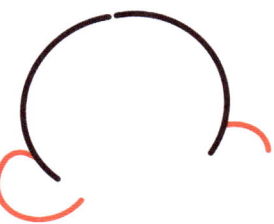

2. At the ends of the open circle, draw two tentacles extending out to the sides.

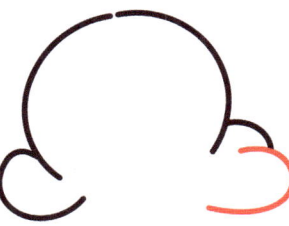

3. Add a tentacle below the right tentacle.

4. Add a larger tentacle below the center of the head/body.

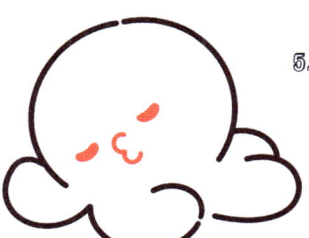

5. Finish with bean-shaped eyes and an E-shaped beak.

GROUCHY THORNBACK COWFISH

1. Draw two upside-down U shapes side by side for the spines on the head.

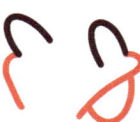

2. Draw a curved line extending down from either end of the U shapes. On the right curved line, draw a semicircle for the eye.

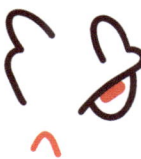

3. Draw a bean-shaped pupil in the eye and a frown between and below the protruding spines.

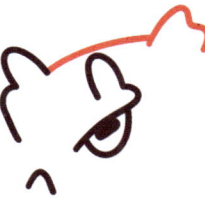

4. Draw a curved line connected to the left spine and an ear-shaped fin at the end.

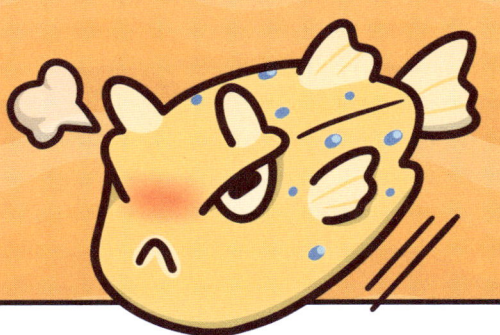

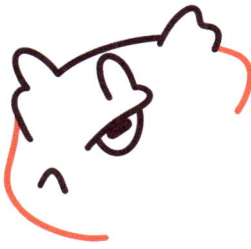

5. Draw the curved line of the face and the end of the body.

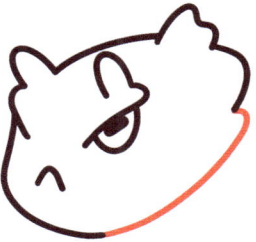

6. Finish the shape of the body by connecting the face and end of the body with a curved line.

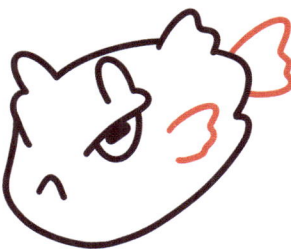

7. Add a winglike arm fin in the center of the body and tail with three peaks.

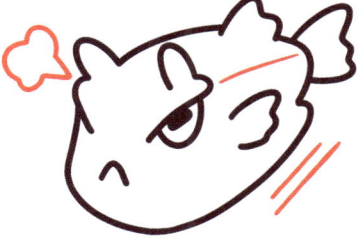

8. Finish with a line from the right eye to the tail, lines along the bottom of the body for movement, and a speech-bubble shape next to the head.

SILLY TURTLE

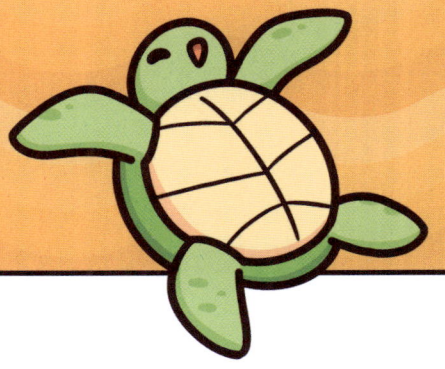

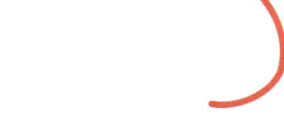

1. Draw a backward C.

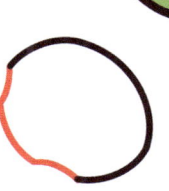

2. Finish out the circular shape with two divots for arms.

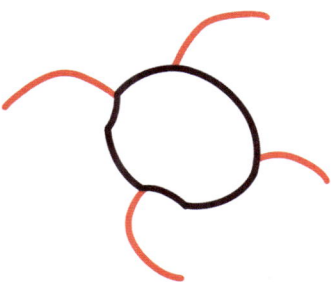

3. Draw four curved lines coming out of each corner of the body, including the divots.

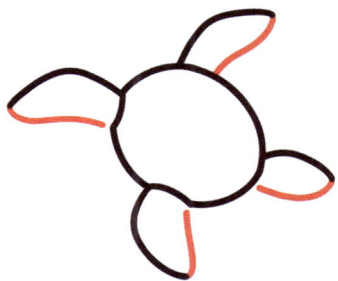

4. Connect the ends of the lines back to the circular body to make paddle-like flippers.

5. Add a half-circle shape at the top of the body and a curved line on the left side of the body and between the legs to add dimension to the shell.

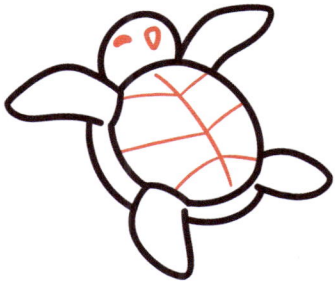

6. Finish with a bean-shaped eye and an open-mouthed smile, and add lines on the shell like a leaf for detail.

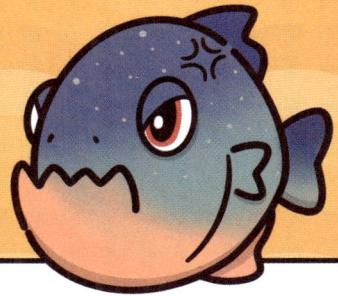

ANGRY PIRHANA

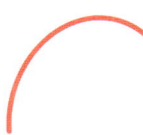

1. Draw a curved line for the top of the head/body.

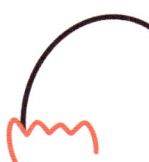

2. Draw the jaw with a jagged line for the sharp teeth.

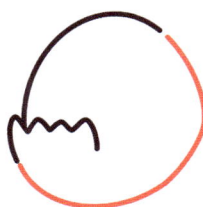

3. Connect the ends of the circle to complete the circular head/body.

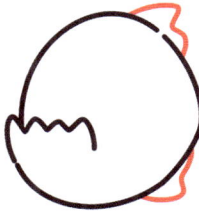

4. Add the top and bottom fins in the shape of a wave.

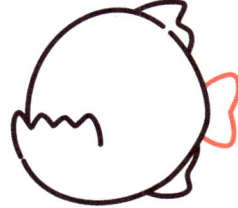

5. Draw the forked tail shaped like an ear.

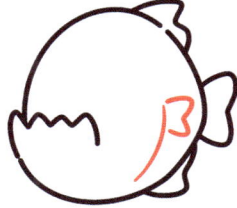

6. Draw the fin near the end of the head/body in a smaller shape of an ear. Add a curved line beside it for the gill.

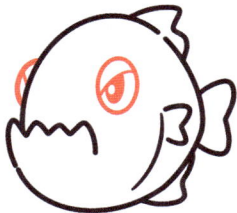

7. Add a circle and semicircle for the eyes. Draw a line to define the the eyelid and a teardrop shape for the iris, leaving a little white for the pupil.

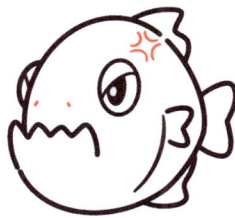

8. Finish with two dots above the jaw for a nose and a tension headache on the forehead with four quarter circles meeting together.

SAD SEAL

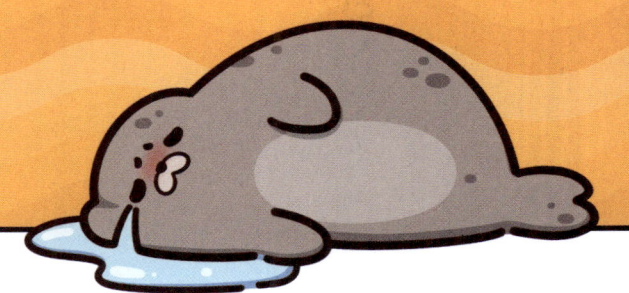

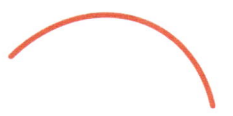

1. Draw a semicircle.

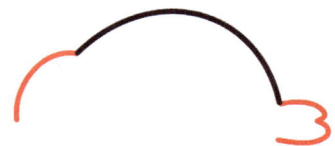

2. Draw a curved line on one end for the head and a tail on the other end shaped like the number three.

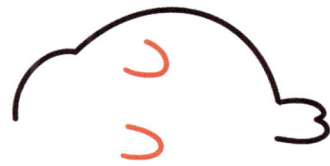

3. Add the two flippers stacked on the center of the body, shaped like backward Cs.

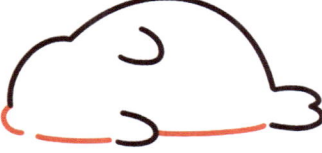

4. Draw a small, curved line at the bottom of the head for the cheek. Add straight lines for the bottom of the body.

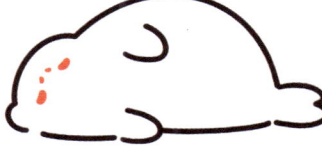

5. Draw bean-shaped eyes and creases in between for a sad face.

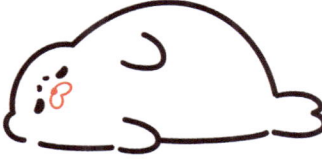

6. Draw the snout between the eyes in the shape of a split four-leaf clover.

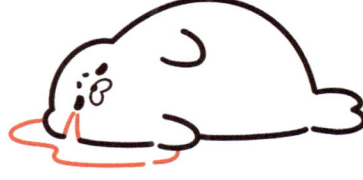

7. Finish with a stream of tears escaping from one eye and pooling around the head.

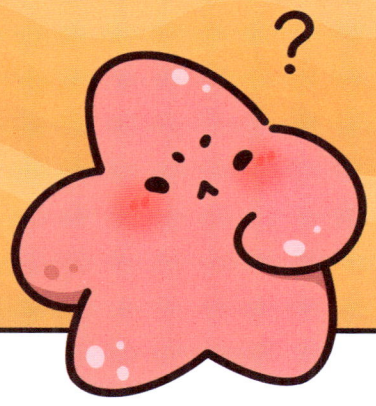

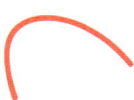

1. Draw the top of an oval at an angle.

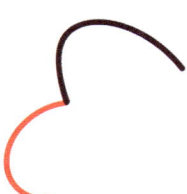

2. Draw a semicircle on the left side of the half oval.

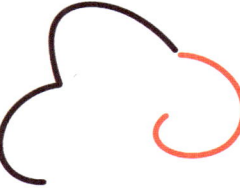

3. Draw a curled line on the right side.

4. Draw the legs with two connected half ovals.

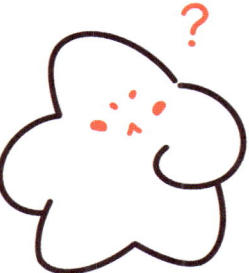

5. Finish with bean-shaped eyes, an upside-down V mouth, and two creases between the eyes. Add a question mark above the head.

SCARED SQUID

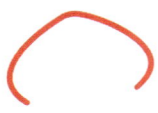

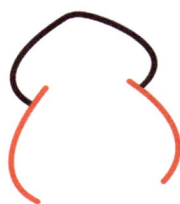

1. Start with a semicircle for the head with a pointed tip.

2. Add two curved lines for each side of the face.

3. Draw two tentacles below either side of the face.

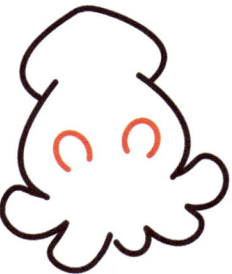

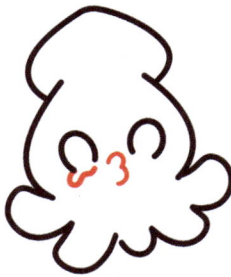

4. Add three tentacles at the bottom of the body with a smaller tentacle in the middle.

5. Draw two unfinished circles in the middle of the head for eyes.

6. Draw a beak as a backward E and add a falling tear at the bottom of one eye.

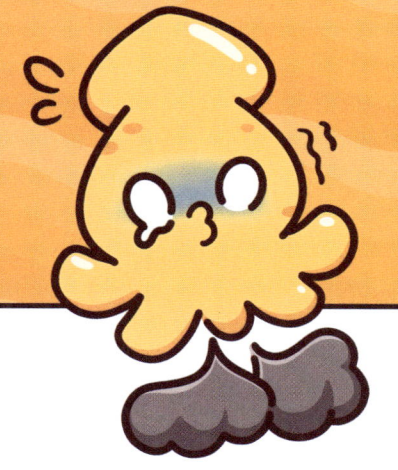

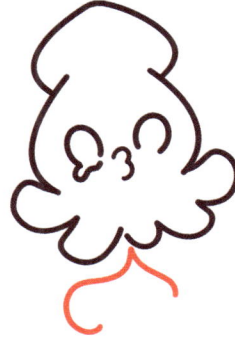

7. Start the ink cloud below the middle tentacle as if starting a dialogue bubble.

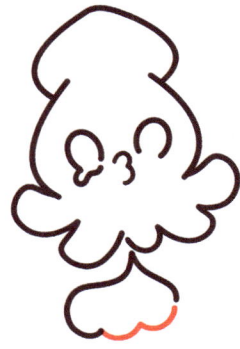

8. Finish the ink cloud with two curved lines like a cloud.

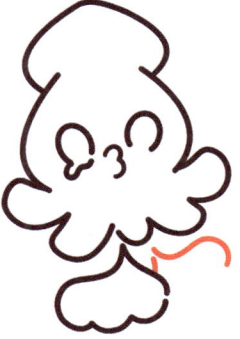

9. Add another start of an ink cloud beside the first cloud.

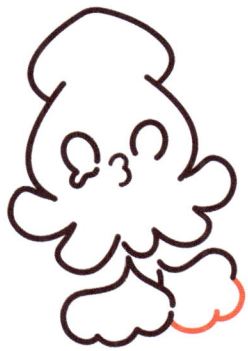

10. Finish the ink cloud with two curved lines like a cloud.

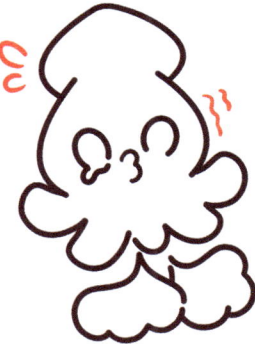

11. Finish with two beads of sweat above and two squiggly lines beside the head.

DAILY ACTIVITIES

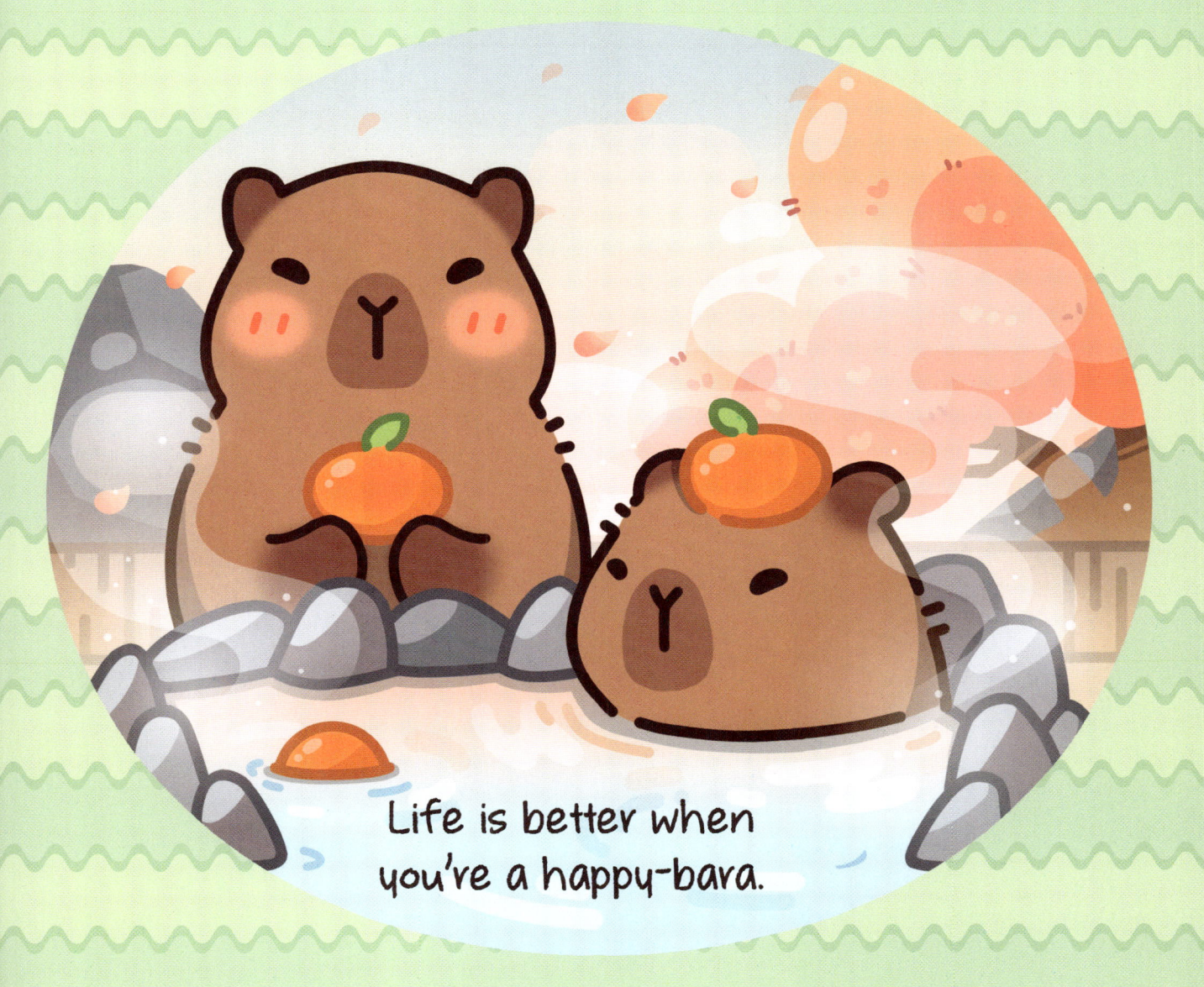

Life is better when
you've a happy-bara.

KING PENGUIN WADDLING

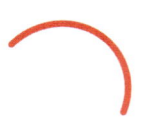

1. Draw a semicircle at an angle for the head.

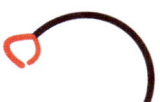

2. On the left side of the semicircle, draw a sideways triangle for the beak.

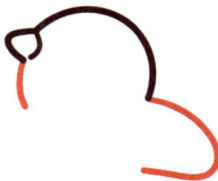

3. Draw a curved line below the beak to finish the head and add a paddle-shaped flipper on the other side.

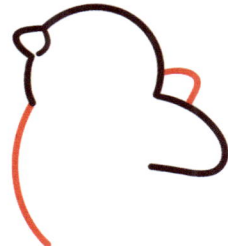

4. Draw a curved line for the stomach. Above the flipper, draw the back flipper in the shape of a backward C.

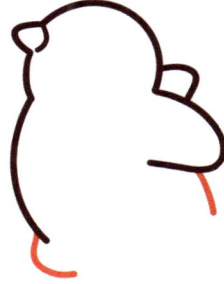

5. Add a short line below the front flipper. Draw the left leg below the stomach.

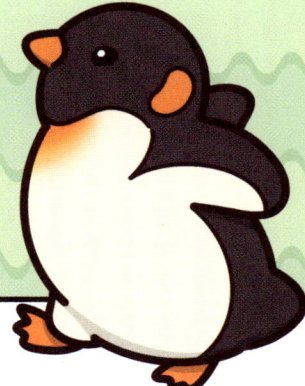

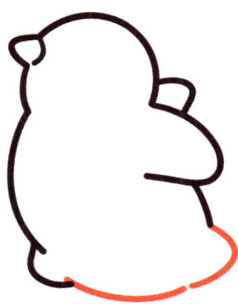

6. Draw a curved line at the bottom of the body and another curved line for the tail.

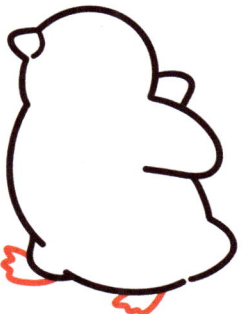

7. Add the webbed feet at the end of the short leg and below the center of the body.

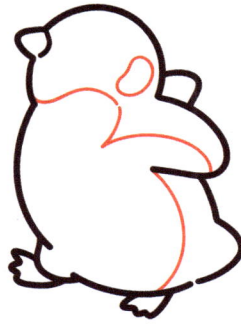

8. Draw a guiding line for coloring. The head and top of the flipper are separated from the stomach and bottom of the flipper. The back and tail are also black. Draw a bean shape where an ear would go.

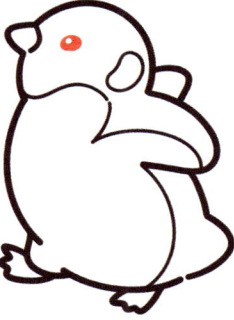

9. Finish with a bean-shaped eye, leaving a little white for the pupil.

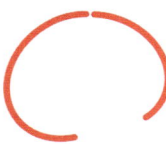

1. Draw a circle with an open bottom.

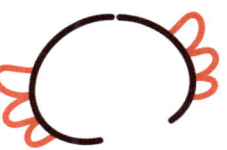

2. Draw three external gills on either side of the circle.

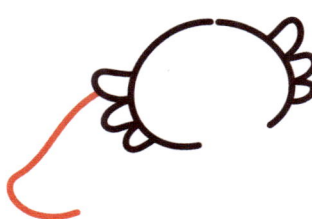

3. Draw a curved line from the top of the left gills to create the tail.

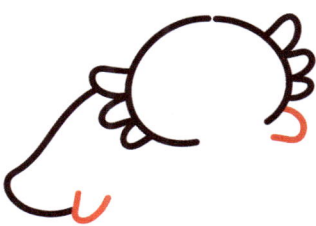

4. Add an arm below the face as a backward C and a leg beside the tail as a U shape.

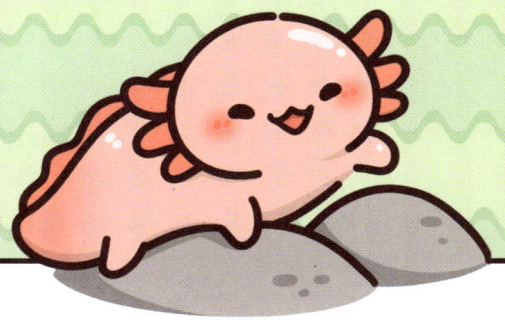

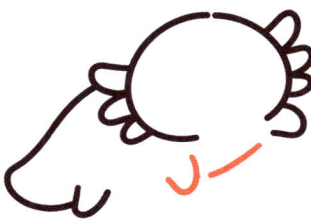

5. Draw an angled line below the face and another arm at the end of the line as a U shape.

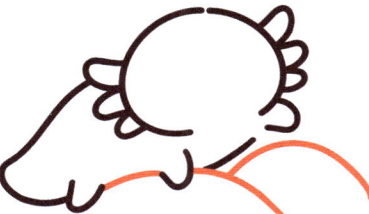

6. Draw two curved lines: one from the back legs to below the right arm and the other below the right arm.

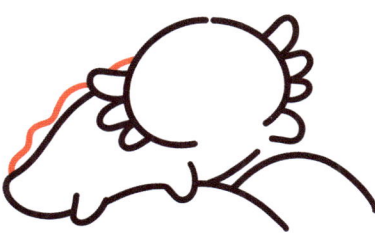

7. Draw the wavy fin on the ridge of the body.

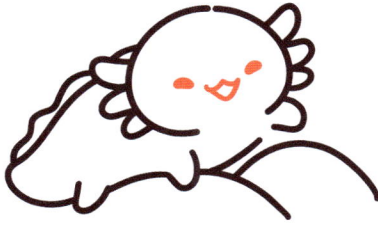

8. Finish with bean-shaped eyes and an open-mouthed smile.

FLYING FISH SOARING

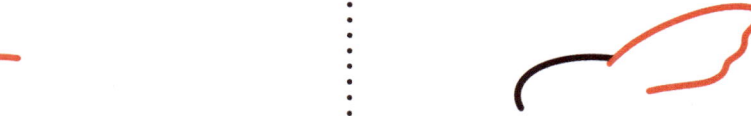

1. Start by drawing a curved line.

2. Draw the front fin in the shape of a wing.

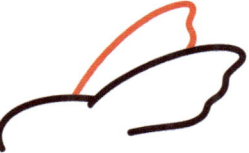

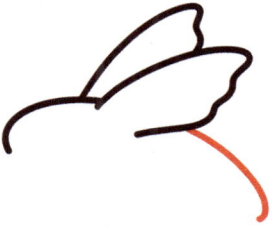

3. Add another fin behind the front fin.

4. Continue the body in a curved line after the winglike fins.

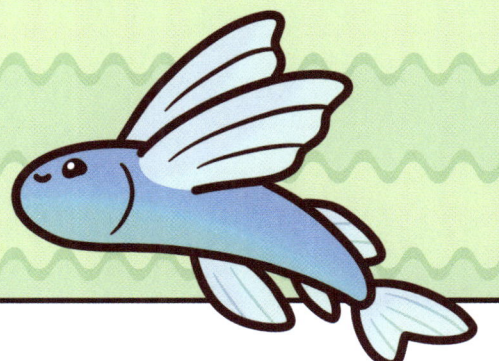

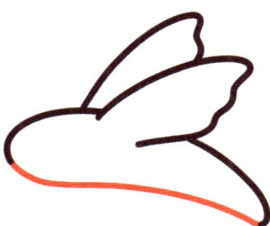

5. Finish the body by connecting the front and back of the body in a curved line.

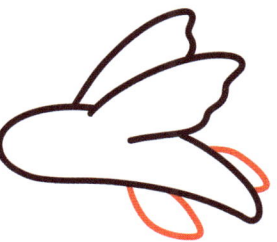

6. Add two smaller fins at the top and bottom of the body after the winglike fins.

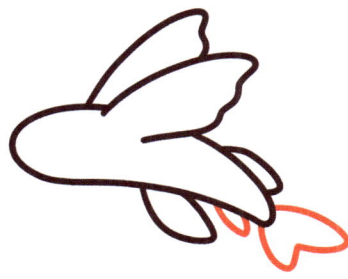

7. Draw a forked tail at the end of the body. Draw an even smaller fin near the tail.

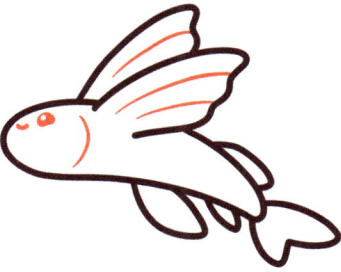

8. Finish with lines on the wing-fins for texture, a curved line on the face for gills, and a happy face, including a bean-shaped eye with a little white pupil and a small smile.

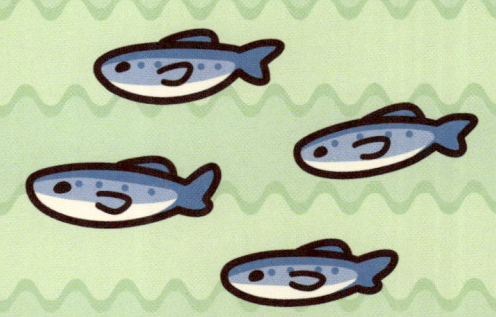

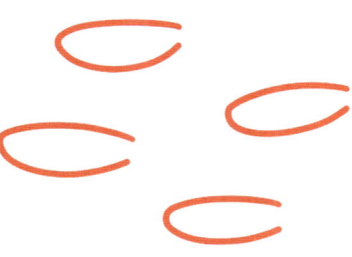

1. Draw four ovals with open ends on the right side.

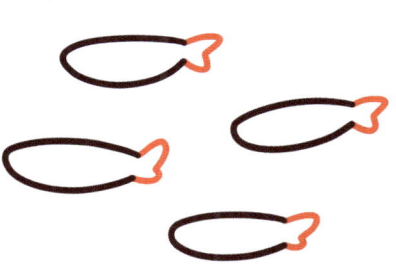

2. Draw a forked tail at the open end of each oval.

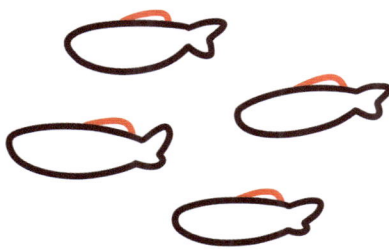

3. Add a curved-line top fin on each fish.

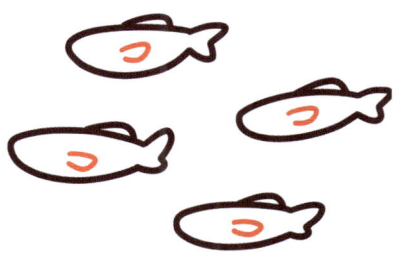

4. Draw a backward C in the center of each body.

5. Finish with a dot on the face of each fish for the eyes.

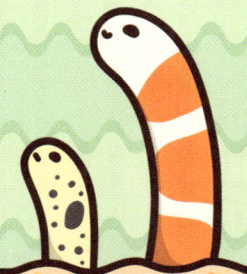

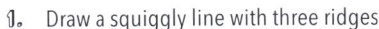

1. Draw a squiggly line with three ridges.

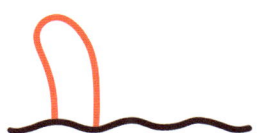

2. Draw a long, rounded shape shooting up from the line.

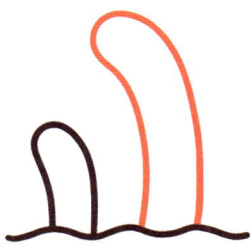

3. Draw an even longer, rounded shape shooting up from the line beside the shorter shape.

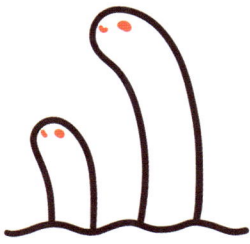

4. Finish with a bean-shaped eye and a small smile on each eel's face.

ELECTRIC EEL CHARGING

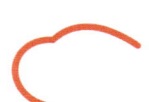

1. Draw a double curved line for the head.

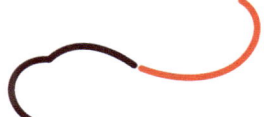

2. Draw a semicircle for the body.

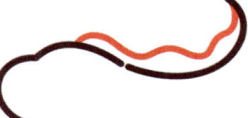

3. Add a wavy fin on top of the body's ridge.

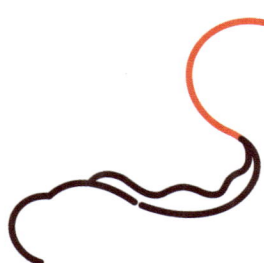

4. Draw another semicircle in the opposite direction.

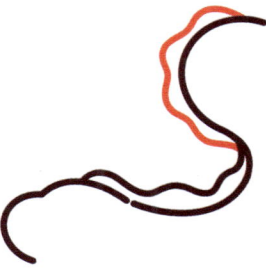

5. Add a wavy fin along the body's ridge.

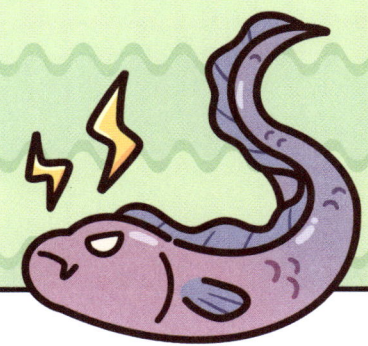

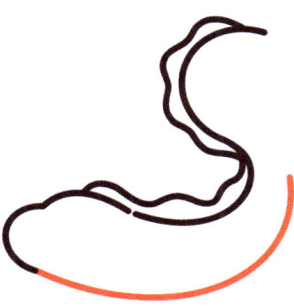

6. Draw a curved line from the head to the middle of the body.

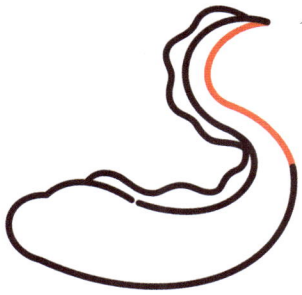

7. Draw a curved line along the body's length to the pointed tip of the tail.

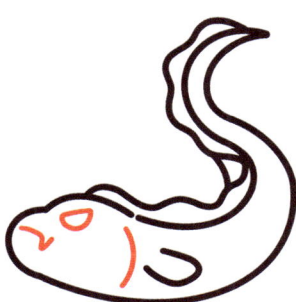

8. Add a curved line for gills, a slanted half-circle shape for the eye, and a line with a sharp tooth for the mouth.

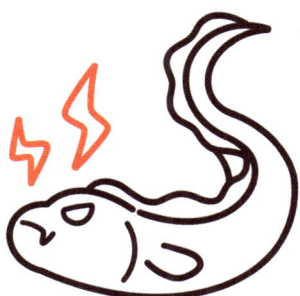

9. Finish with two lightning bolts above the head.

STINGRAY ATTACKING

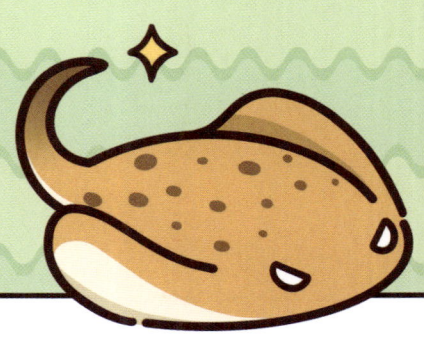

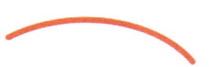

1. Draw a curved line.

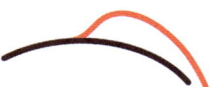

2. Draw a fin in a wave shape starting in the center of the curved line.

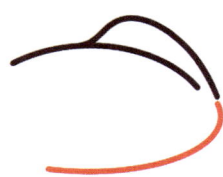

3. Connect the fin to the curved line of the face.

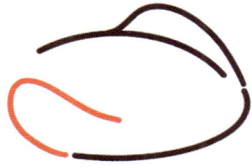

4. Add a paddle-like fin next to the face.

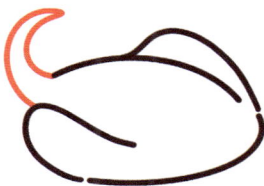

5. Draw a pointed, curved tail at the end of the body.

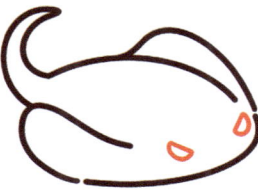

6. Draw two eyes in half-circle shapes for an angry face.

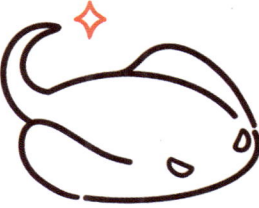

7. Finish with a diamond shape above the tail for the sting attack.

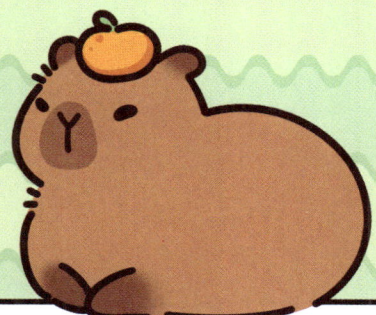

CAPYBARA CHILLING

1. Draw a small oval for the orange that will sit on the capybara's head.

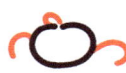

2. Add a stem to the oval, then draw the ears on either side of the orange.

3. Draw the sides of the face with curved lines, making the left side longer for a cheek. Add fur texture below the left ear.

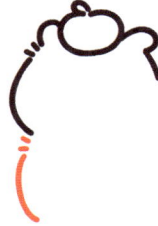

4. Draw the front of the body with a curved line and more fur texture below the cheek.

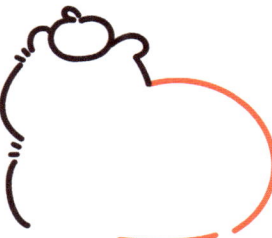

5. Draw the rest of the body with a semicircle. Add the bottom of the body off the backside with a slightly curved line.

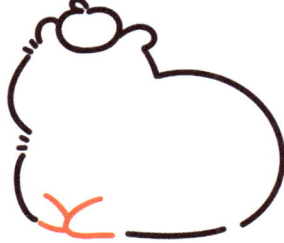

6. Draw an arm with an inward U shape and then another arm that touches the first in the opposite direction.

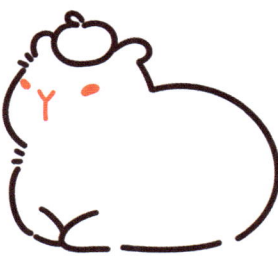

7. Finish with bean-shaped eyes and a Y-shaped nose and mouth.

YELLOWHEAD JAWFISH MOUTH-BROODING

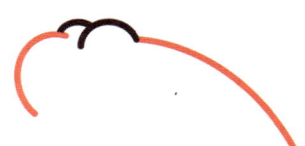

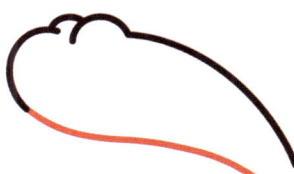

1. Draw a semicircle connected to a smaller curved line.

2. Draw the curved line of the mouth and a longer, flatter curved line of the body.

3. Draw the bottom of the body with a curved line.

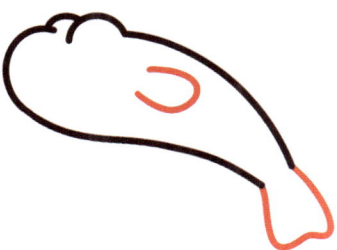

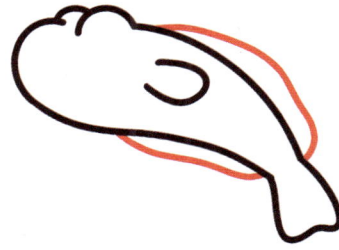

4. Add a forked tail and a backward C fin in the middle of the body.

5. Add wavy-lined fins to the top and bottom of the body, starting at the arm fin and ending before the tail.

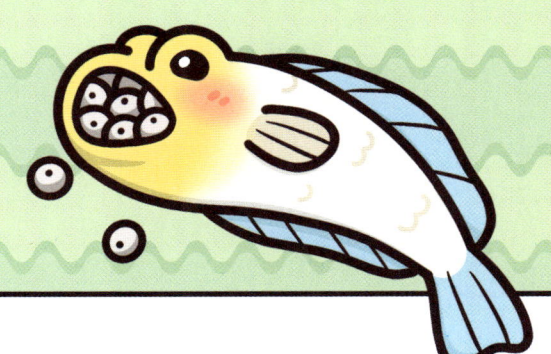

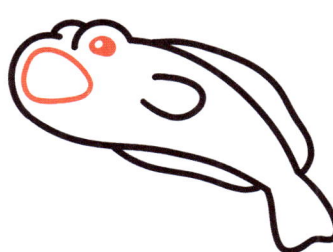

6. Add a bean-shaped eye, leaving a little white for the pupil, and a circular open mouth.

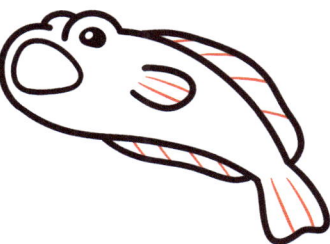

7. Draw texture lines on the fins and tail.

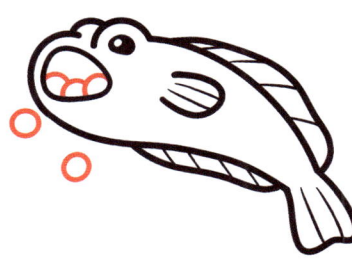

8. Draw semicircles along the bottom of the mouth and circles around the face.

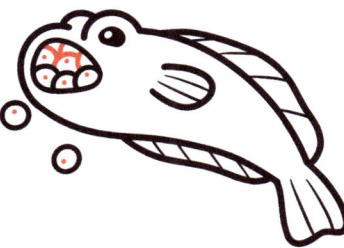

9. Finish by filling up the rest of the mouth with semicircles and adding dots in the circles. These eggs are their babies.

SHARK HUNTING

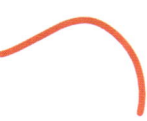

1. Draw the curved line of the face.

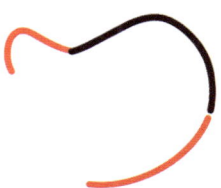

2. Draw the pointed fin and the curved line of the stomach.

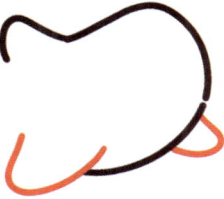

3. Add the paddle-like arm fins on either side of the body.

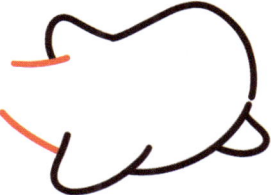

4. Draw two lines to the left of the fins.

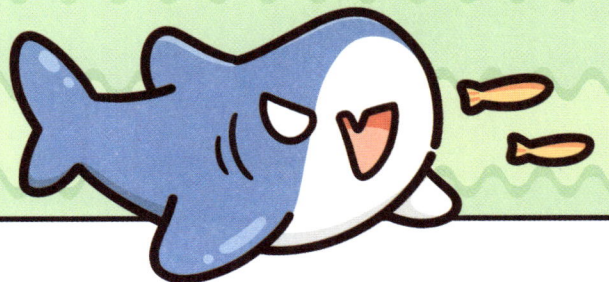

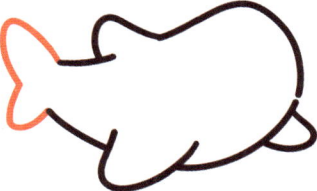

5. Draw a tail at the end of the body in the shape of an ear.

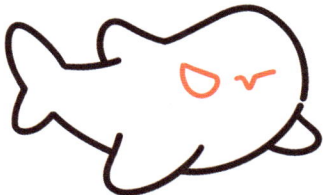

6. Add a half-circle shape for the eye and a straight line with a sharp tooth for the mouth.

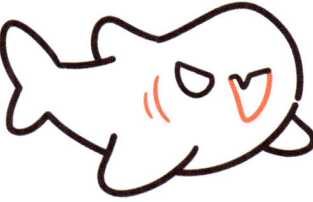

7. Add two lines beside the eye for gills and a curved line for an open mouth.

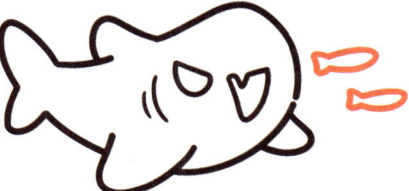

8. Finish with two fish shapes ahead of the shark's mouth.

HERMIT CRAB COMING HOME

1. Draw two ovals side by side with open bottoms.

2. Add two filled-in circles at the bottom of the ovals, with an open, triangular mouth beneath the eyes.

3. Draw two mirrored semicircles with straight lines halfway through each center.

4. Add a curved line to each semicircle to create two claws.

5. Draw a swirl next to the right claw, partially hidden by the claw.

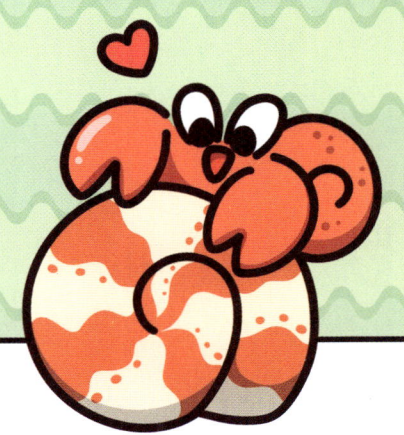

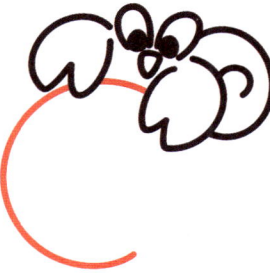

6. Draw a half circle below the claws.

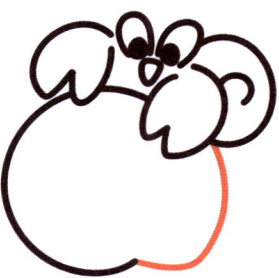

7. Add a curved line below the right claw to close out the circular shape.

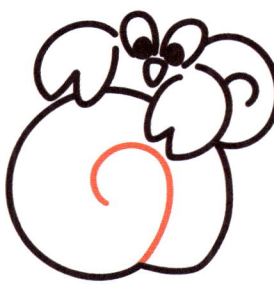

8. Draw a swirl in the center of the circle.

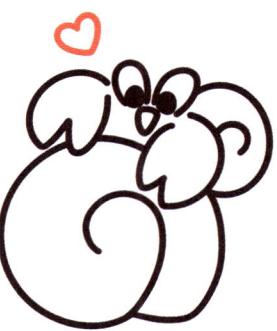

9. Finish with a heart above the eyes.

KOI SWIMMING

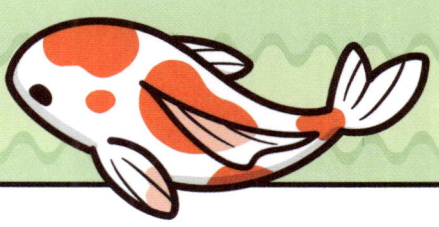

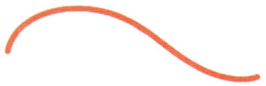
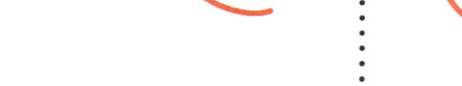

1. Draw a curved line in the shape of a half infinity sign.

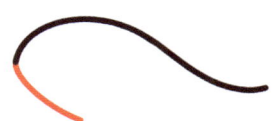

2. Add the front of the face with a shorter line.

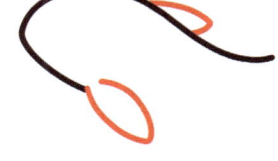

3. Draw a thin fin below the face, then draw another thin fin above and behind the body.

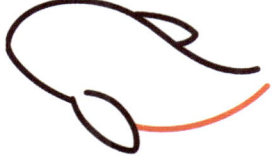

4. Draw a curved line from the front fin to almost meet the top of the body.

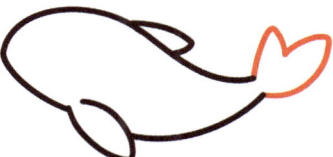

5. Add a forked tail.

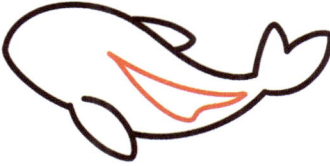

6. Draw a line through the body, following the curve of the body. Below the line, add the shape of a fin.

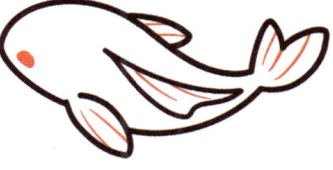

7. Finish with a half-circle eye and lines on the fins and tail for texture.

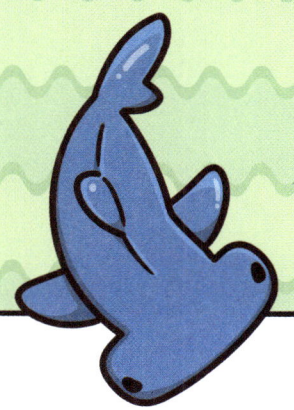

HAMMERHEAD SHARK DIVING

1. Start with a forked tail in the shape of a mitten.

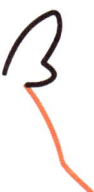

2. Draw one side of the body with a slightly bent line.

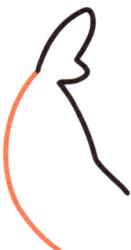

3. Draw the other side of the body with a curved line.

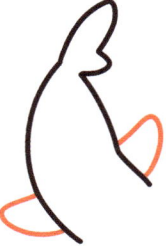

4. Draw fins on either side of the body.

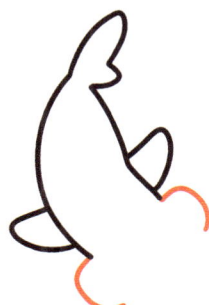

5. Draw the sides of the head at the end of the body in the shape of parentheses.

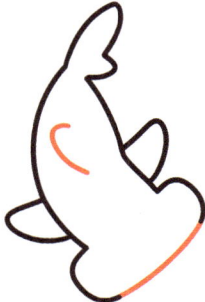

6. Connect the ends of the parentheses to finish the head. Add a C-shaped fin in the center of the body.

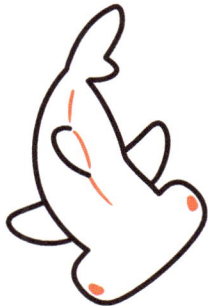

7. Finish with bean-shaped eyes on opposite ends of the head and a line through the spine of the shark for dimension.

FROG LEAPING

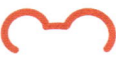

1. Start with the eyes and top of the frog's head. Draw two unfinished circles connected by a short line.

2. Draw the curved line of the frog's head.

3. Draw the top of the body with a curved line.

4. Draw the arms with two parallel, curved lines on either side of the head.

5. Add the webbed hands at the ends of the arms.

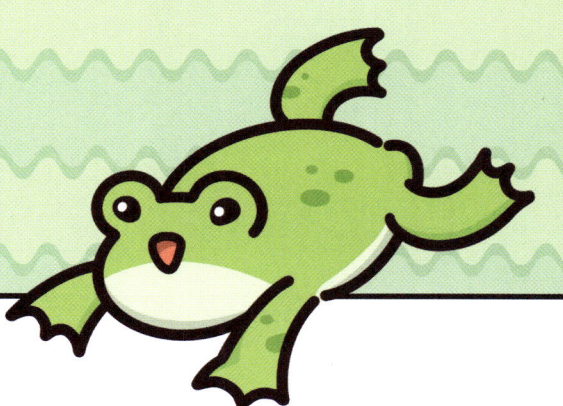

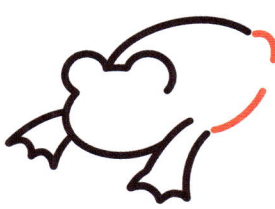

6. Add the tail with the short, curved line at the end of the body. Draw the bottom of the body with a curved line.

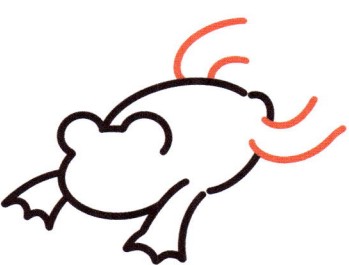

7. Draw the legs with two parallel, curved lines on either side of the tail.

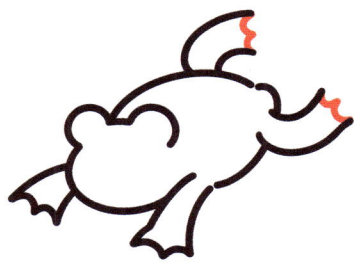

8. Add the webbed feet at the ends of the legs.

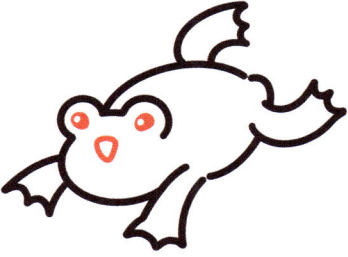

9. Finish with bean-shaped eyes, leaving white for pupils, and an open, happy mouth.

CLAM HIDING

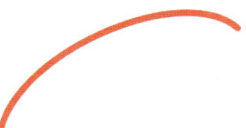

1. Draw a curved line at an angle.

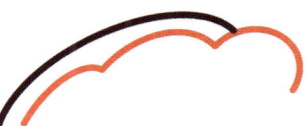

2. Draw three curved lines in a row like the top of a cloud.

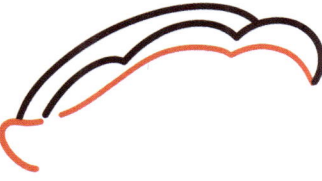

3. Draw two connected, curved lines below the other two lines, with the left line longer than the right. Draw a semicircle to the left of the lines.

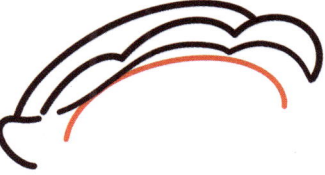

4. Draw a semicircle below.

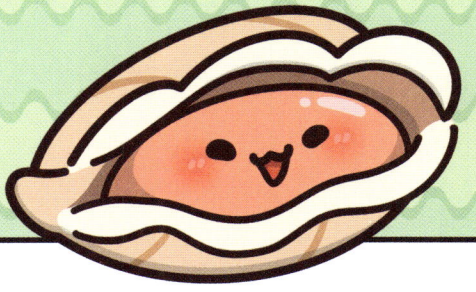

5. Draw a curved line with a dip in the middle.

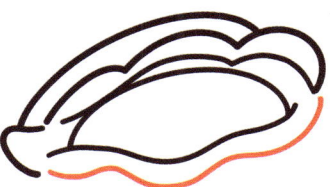

6. Draw a wavy line below with a dip in the middle again.

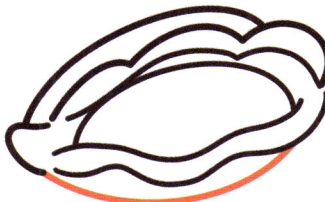

7. Draw a curved line closing out the clam's shape.

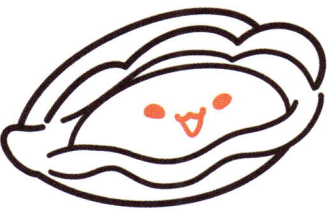

8. Finish with bean-shaped eyes and an open-mouthed smile.

WHALE SPOUTING

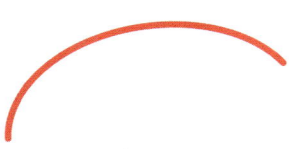

1. Draw a curved line.

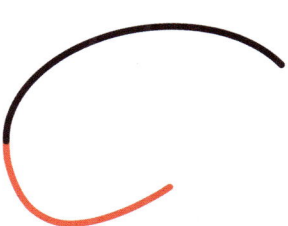

2. Draw a curved corner for the mouth.

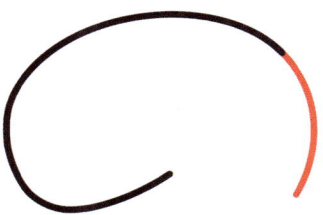

3. Add a curved line for the tail.

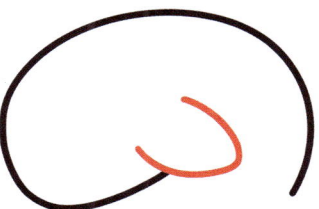

4. Draw a backward-C fin starting from the center of the body.

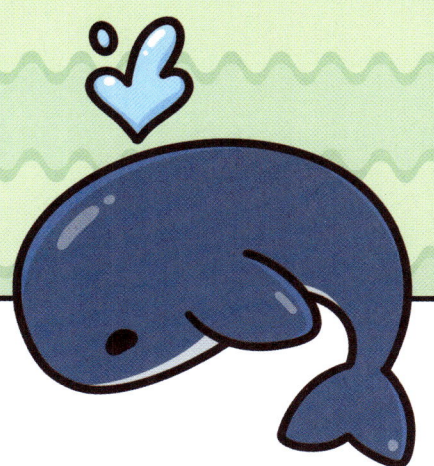

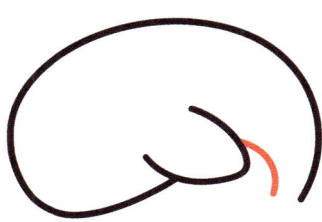

5. Draw a short, curved line from the fin to the end of the body.

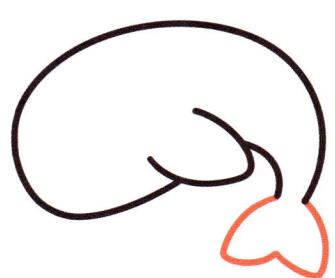

6. Draw a forked tail.

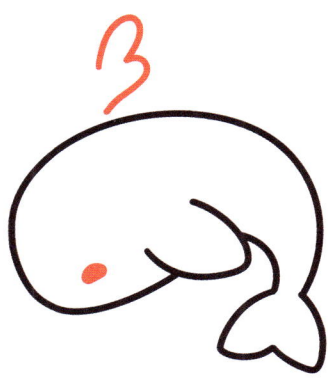

7. Add a bean-shaped eye on the lower face and a winglike line above the head/body.

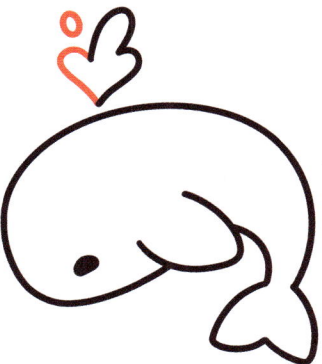

8. Finish with a half heart connecting to the wing shape, with a circle above for the waterspout.

BABY SWIMMERS

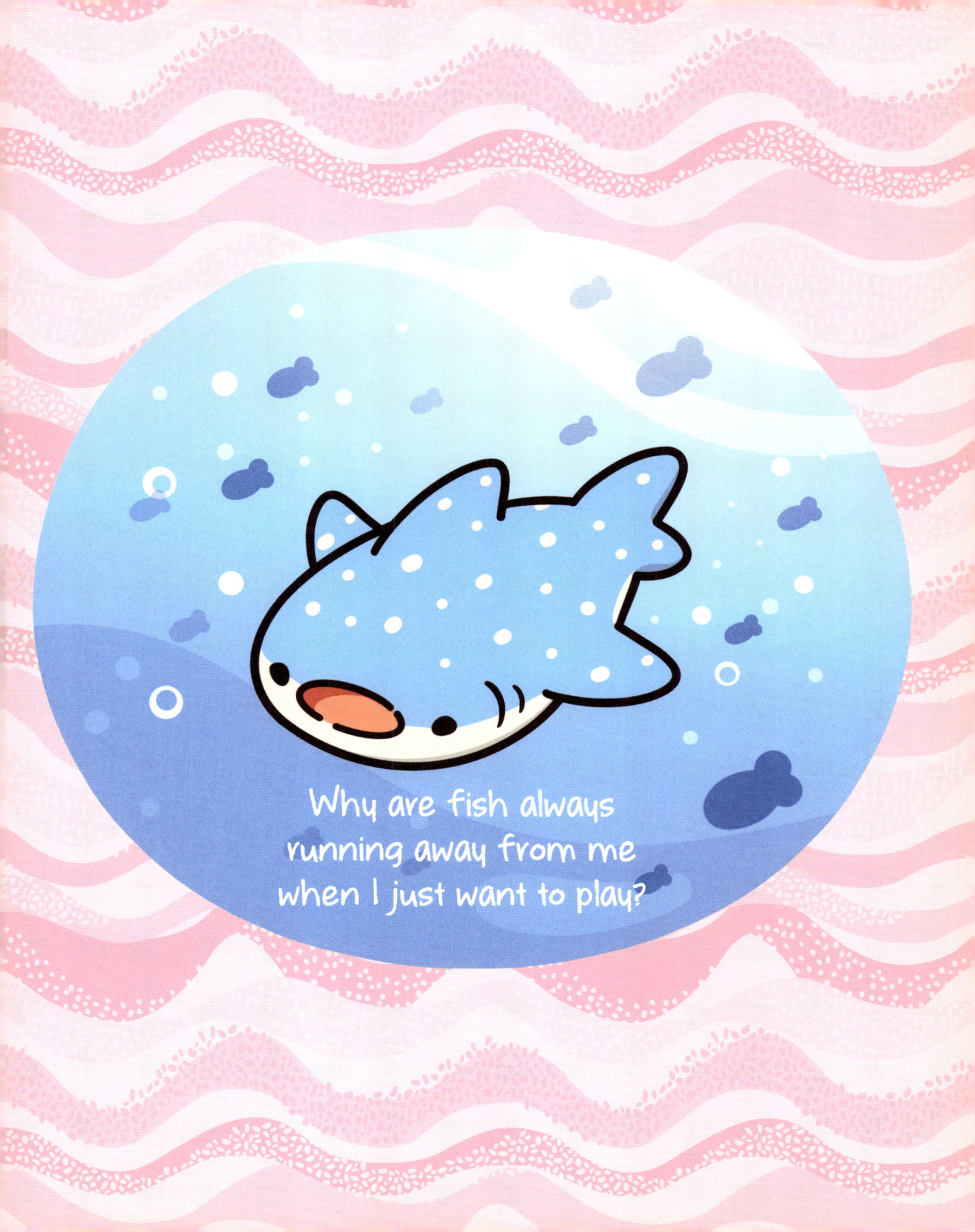

PUFFIN

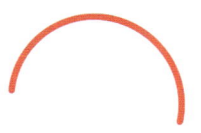

1. Draw a semicircle.

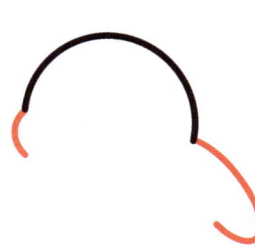

2. Draw a small, curved line for the cheek and a paddle-like wing on the other side.

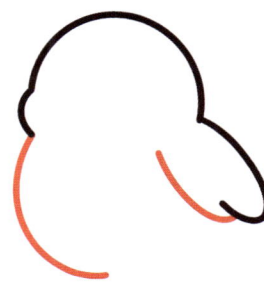

3. Draw a curved line for the stomach and add a curved line to the wing.

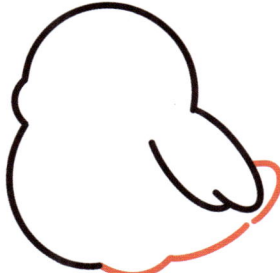

4. Draw a short, curved line below the stomach. Draw a curved line past the wing for the tail.

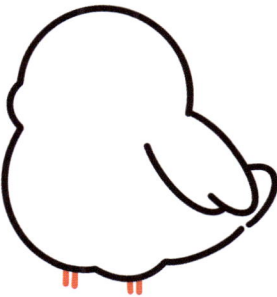

5. Add two short, parallel lines beneath the body for legs.

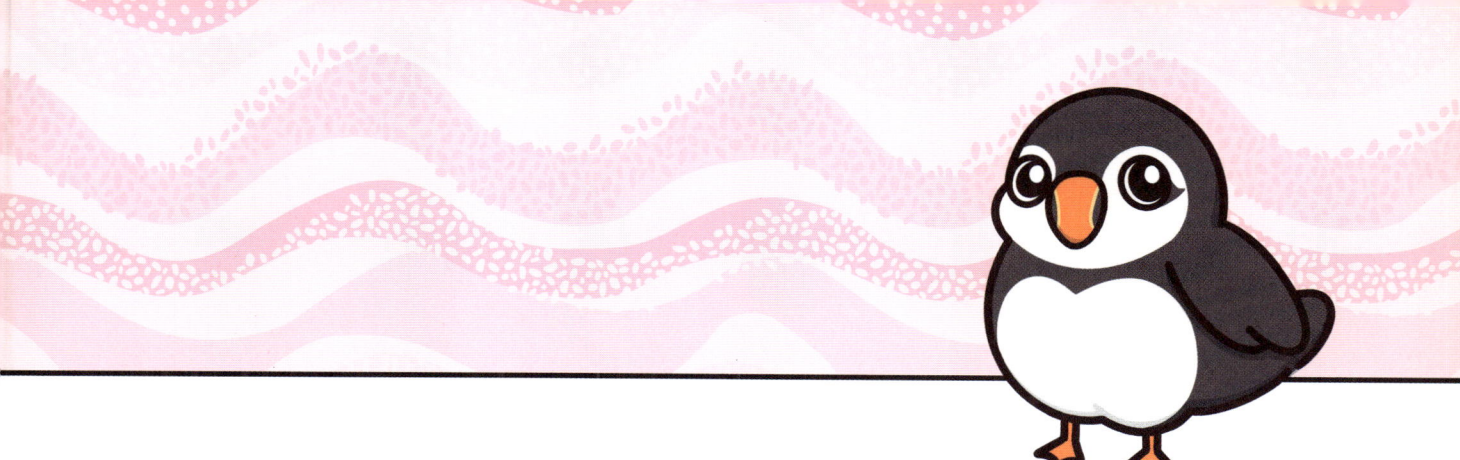

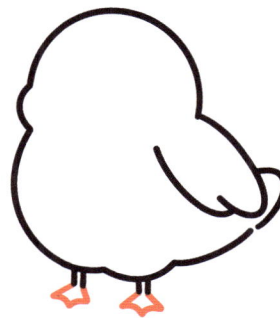

6. Add webbed feet at the end of each leg.

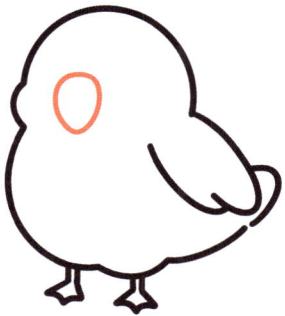

7. Draw an upside-down egg beside the cheek for the beak.

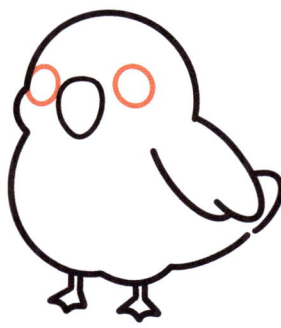

8. Draw two circles on either side of the beak for the eyes.

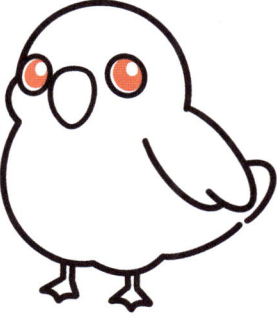

9. Finish by almost completely filling in the circles for the irises, leaving small, open circles for pupils.

SEA URCHIN

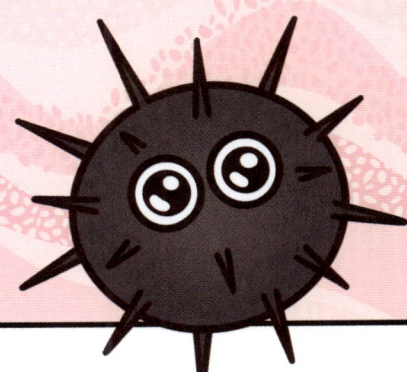

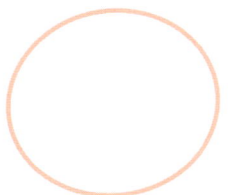

1. Pencil a guiding circle.

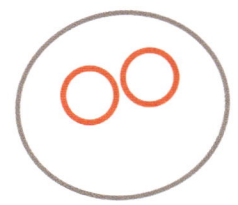

2. Draw two circles side by side in the penciled circle for the eyes.

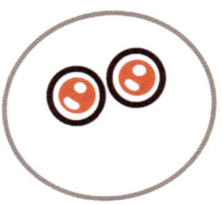

3. Fill in the eyes with round irises, leaving white for pupils and shine.

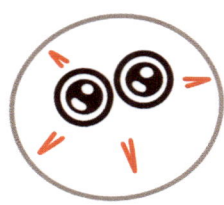

4. Draw points or V shapes fanning out from the eyes.

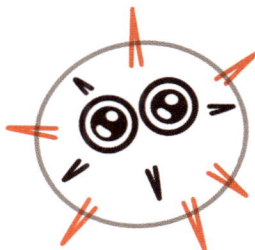

5. Draw longer points or V shapes for the spines, fanning out from just inside the penciled circle.

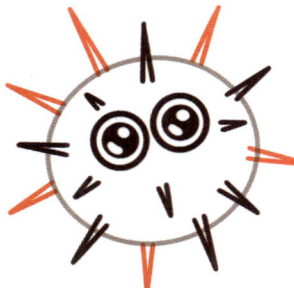

6. Draw longer spines fanning out from the edge of the penciled circle.

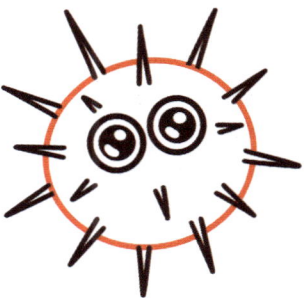

7. Erase the pencil lines inside the spines, then finish by drawing over the remaining lines of the guiding circle.

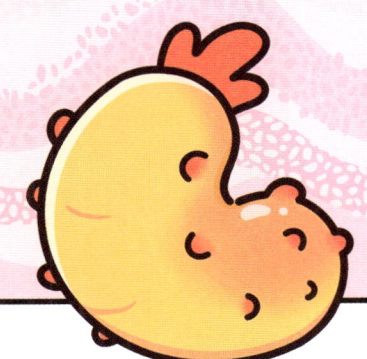

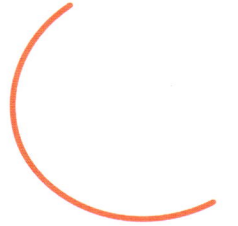

1. Draw a semicircle at an angle.

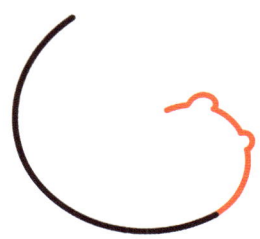

2. Draw a semicircle connected to one end and half the size. Add two small, semicircular bumps for ears.

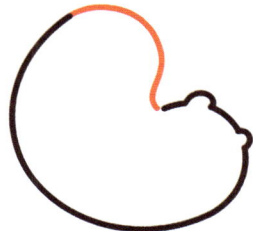

3. Add a curved line connecting the end of the body to the head to complete the shape.

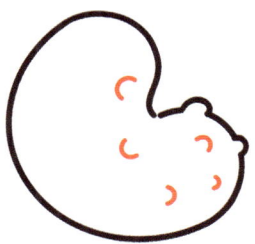

4. Add semicircular lines on the face at different angles.

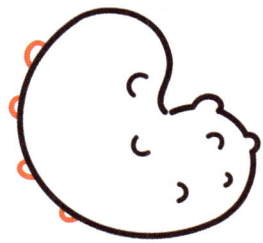

5. Add semicircular lines along the edge of the body.

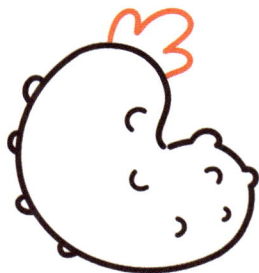

6. Finish with a three-pointed, cactus-shaped top.

BLUE TANG

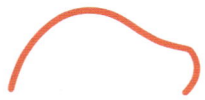

1. Draw a curved line with a turn at the end.

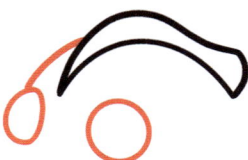

2. Draw a semicircle below the curved line and connected to each end.

3. Draw a curved line connected to an oval for the left eye. Add a circle beneath the fin for the other eye.

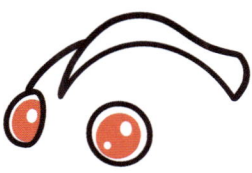

4. Fill in the eyes with round irises, leaving white for pupils and shine.

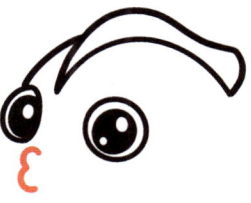

5. Add an E-shaped mouth below the left eye.

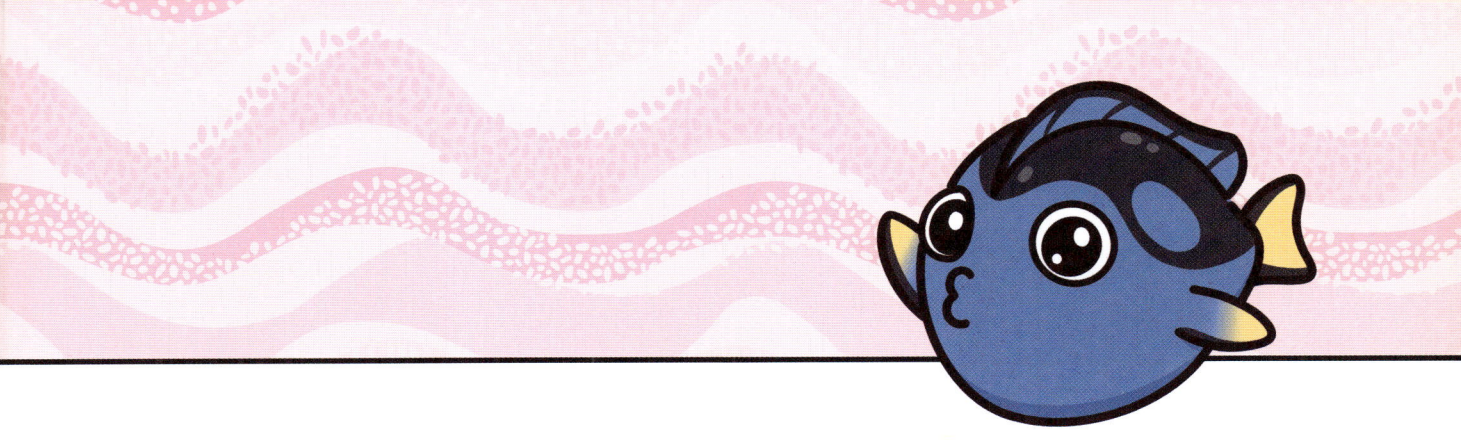

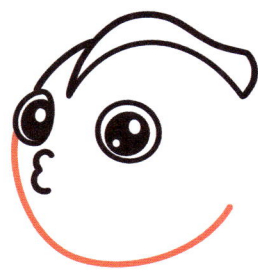

6. Draw a semicircle to almost complete the circular head/body.

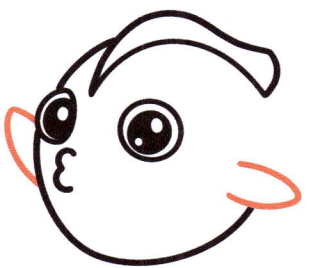

7. Draw paddle-like fins on either side of the head/body.

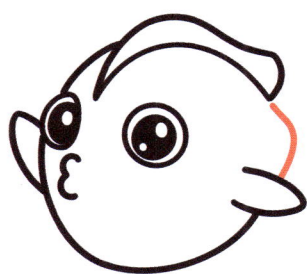

8. Add a curved line from the top fin to the right fin to close off the shape.

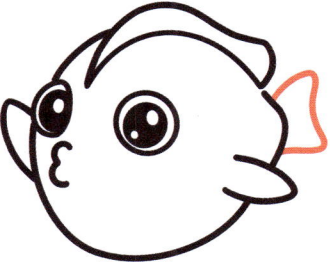

9. Finish with a slightly forked tail.

GOLDFISH

1. Draw a small circle for the eye.

2. Fill in the eye with a round iris, leaving white for the pupil and shine.

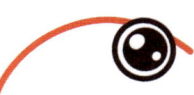

3. Draw a curved line through and past the eye.

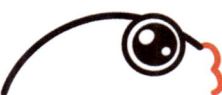

4. Add a mouth shaped like the number three.

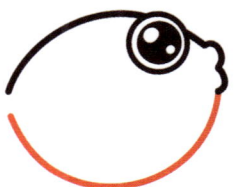

5. Draw a semicircle for the bottom of the body.

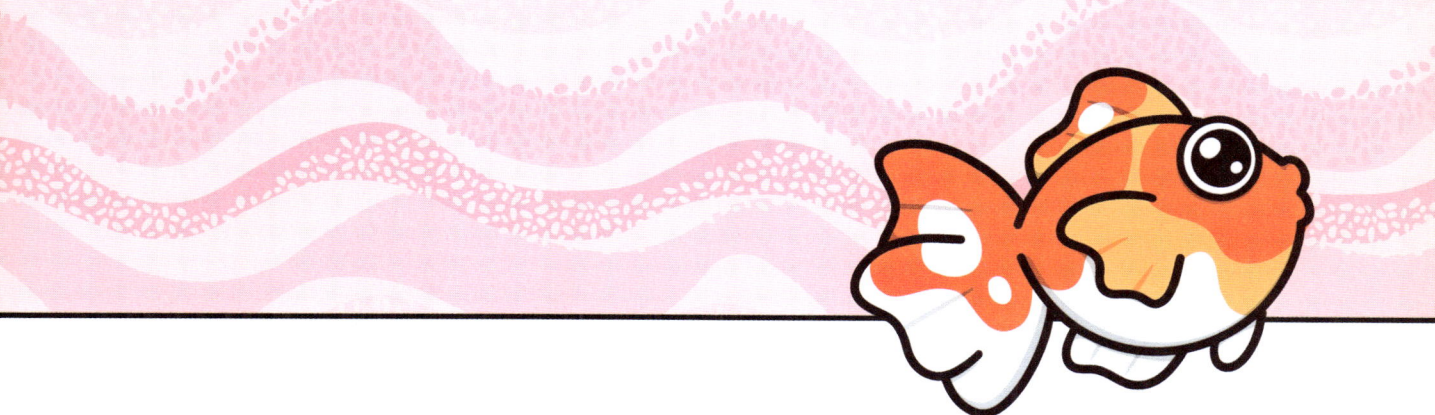

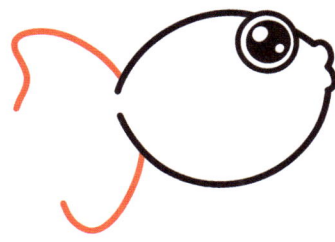

6. Draw the top of the tail like a shark fin and the bottom of the tail with a curved line.

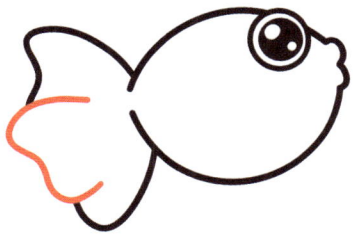

7. Connect the bottom and top of the tail with an ear-shaped line.

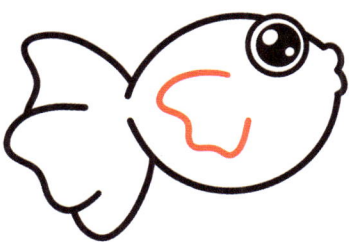

8. Draw a winglike fin in the center of the body.

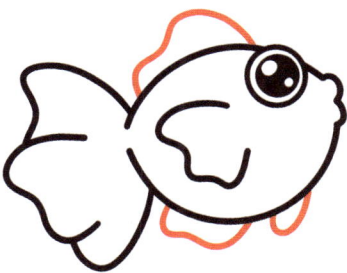

9. Finish with a wavy fin on top, a small fin below the eye, and a wavy fin below the side fin.

SEA SLUG

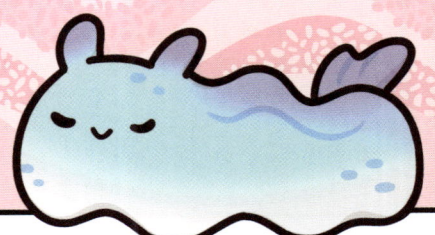

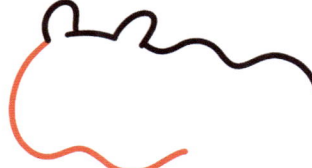

1. Draw two upside down U shapes side by side for the rhinophores on the head.

2. Add a line connecting the rhinophores.

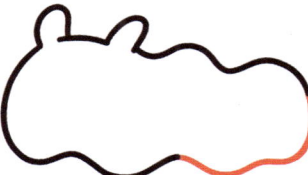

3. Draw a wavy line to the right of the rhinophores.

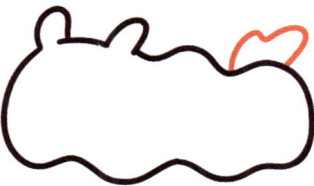

4. Draw a curved line that turns into a wavy line for the face.

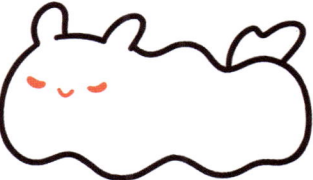

5. Draw a wavy line connecting the top and bottom of the body.

6. Draw a tail as a sideways three at the end of the body.

7. Finish by drawing bean-shaped eyes and a small smile.

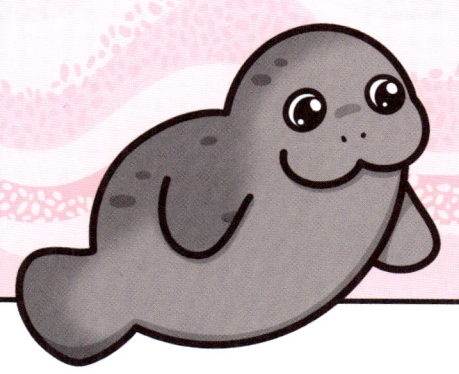

MANATEE

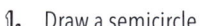

1. Draw a semicircle.

2. Connect a semicircle to the left of the head and draw a sideways three below the head.

3. Draw a curved line for the stomach leading to a C-shaped tail.

4. Add a U-shaped flipper in the middle of the body and a flipper on the right side of the body.

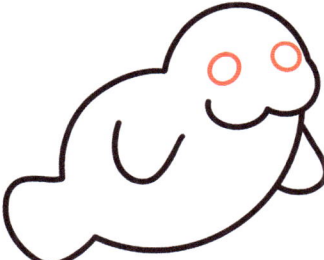

5. Add two circles on either side of the face for the eyes.

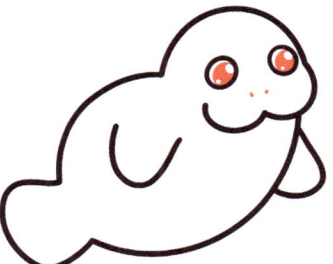

6. Finish by almost completely filling the eyes with the irises, leaving white for pupils and shine, and add two dots below for the nose.

HERMIT CRAB

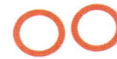

1. Draw two circles side by for the eyes.

2. Almost completely fill in the eyes with the irises, leaving white for the pupils and shine. Add a small smile in between the eyes.

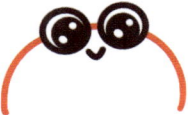

3. Draw a semicircle by connecting the eyes with a straight line and curved lines on either side of the face.

4. Add two mitten-shaped claws beneath the face.

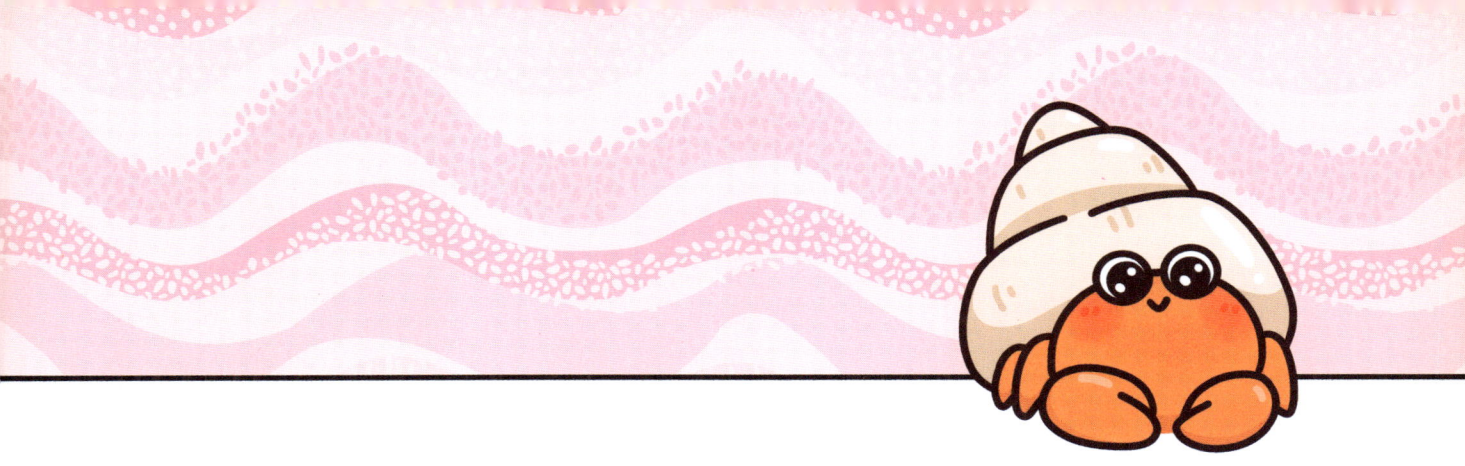

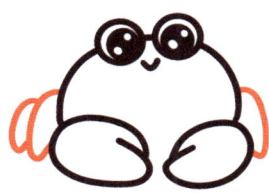

5. Draw two pointed legs on the left side and one pointed leg on the other beside the claws.

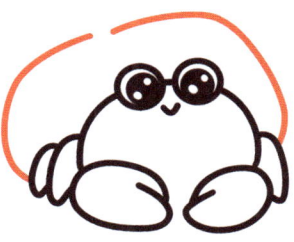

6. Draw two curved lines meeting over the top of the head in a trapezoid shape.

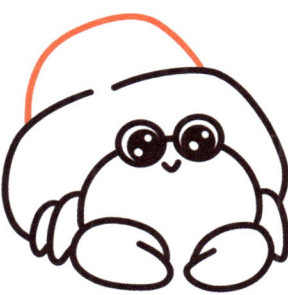

7. Draw a smaller trapezoid shape on top.

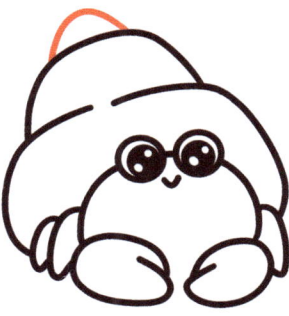

8. Finish with a small triangle to top the shell.

DUMBO OCTOPUS

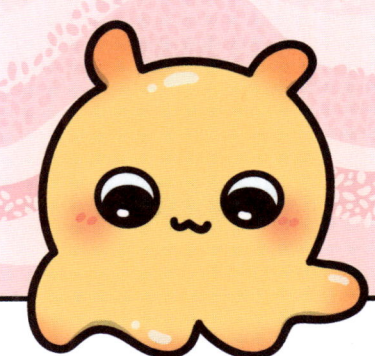

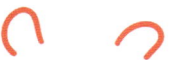

1. Draw two upside-down U shapes side by side.

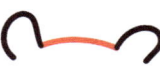

2. Draw a curved line to connect the U shapes.

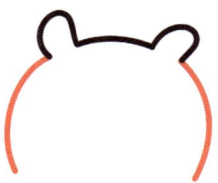

3. Draw curved lines on either side of the face.

4. Add a curvy line on one end.

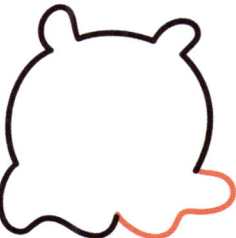

5. Add a curvy line on the other end to close the shape.

6. Add two circles on the head/body for the eyes.

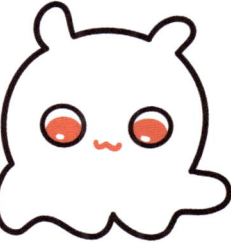

7. Finish by drawing in the irises, leaving white for the pupils, and adding a sideways E-shaped mouth.

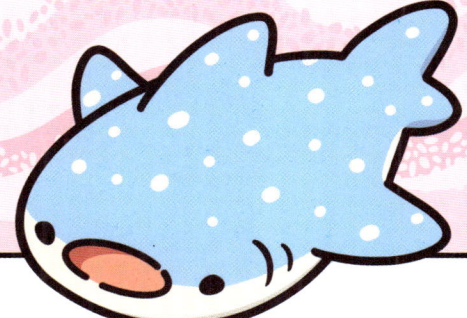

WHALE SHARK

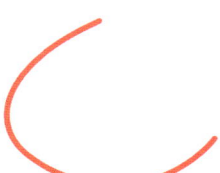

1. Draw a semicircle.

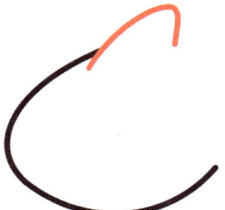

2. Add an angular fin on the top.

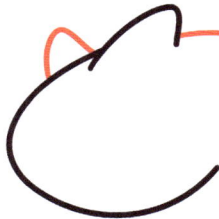

3. Add another angular fin on the left side of the body, and draw a short, curved line after the top fin.

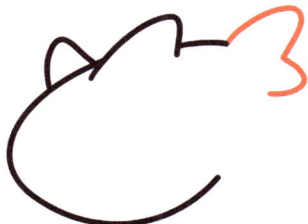

4. Draw an ear-shaped tail at the end of the body.

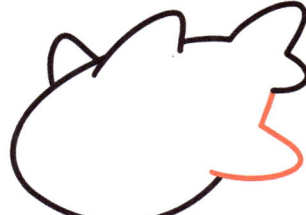

5. Draw a paddle-like fin on the right side of the body and connect the fin to the tail with a straight line.

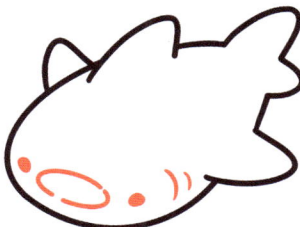

6. Finish by adding a long and open mouth, circular eyes on either side of the mouth, and two curved lines to the right of the face for the gills.

PUFFERFISH

1. Draw five upside-down V shapes in a semicircular shape for the spines.

2. Draw the top of the circle, connecting the spines.

3. Add the nose and a backward-C fin in the center of the body.

4. Draw the bottom of the head/body to almost finish the circular shape.

5. Add the tail in the shape of a backward C.

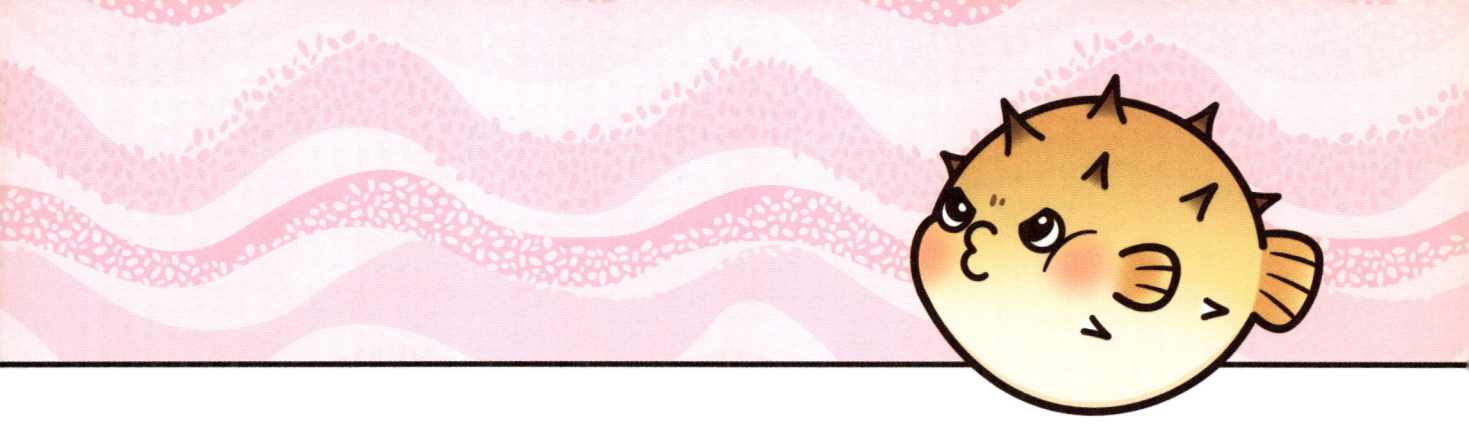

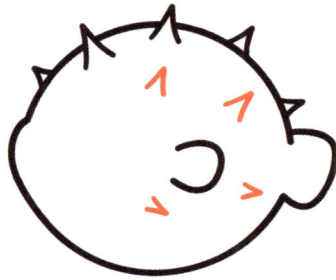

6. Add more V spikes around the fin.

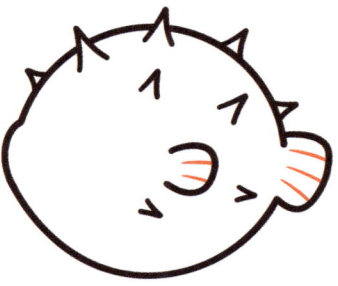

7. Add lines on the fin and tail for texture.

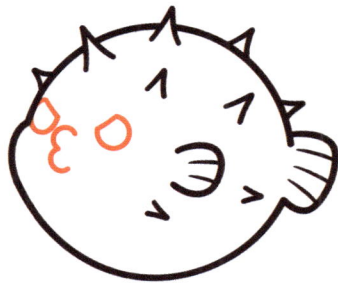

8. Draw the face with the mouth as an E and circular eyes with flat tops for an angry face.

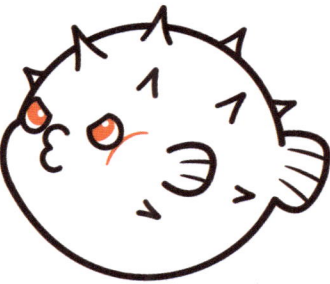

9. Finish with a crease below one eye to define the puffy cheek, and partially color in the eyes for the irises, leaving white for the pupils.

CUTTLEFISH

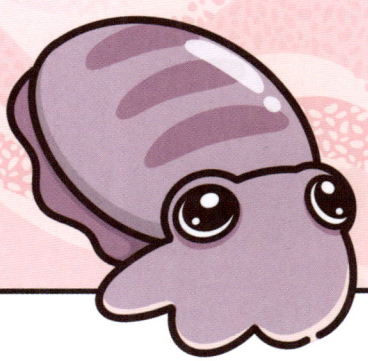

1. Draw two circles side by side for the eyes.

2. Almost completely fill in the eyes for the irises, leaving white for pupils and shine.

3. Draw semicircles around each of the eyes.

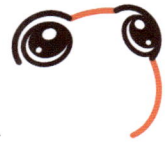

4. Connect the semicircles with a straight line between the eyes and add a curved line below the eyes on the right side for the cheek.

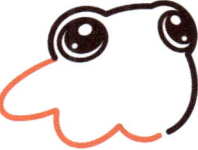

5. Draw three curved lines in a row like a cloud to complete the shape of the face.

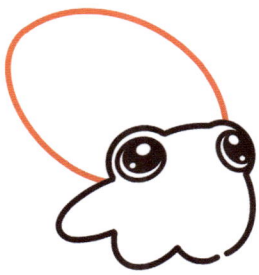

6. Behind the face, draw an egg shape at an angle.

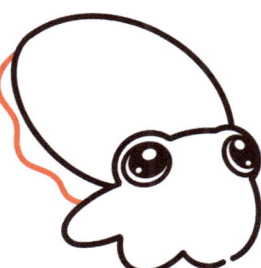

7. Finish with a wavy line along the left side of the body.

FROG

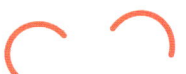

1. Draw two semicircles at an angle.

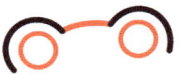

2. Add a curved line connecting the semicircles, and draw circles within for the eyes.

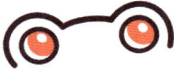

3. Almost completely fill in the eyes for the irises, leaving white for the pupils.

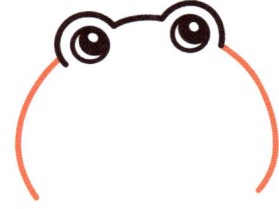

4. Add two curved lines on either side of the head/body.

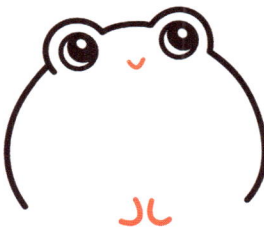

5. Finish with two U shapes at an angle for the hands and a little smile between the eyes.

MOLA

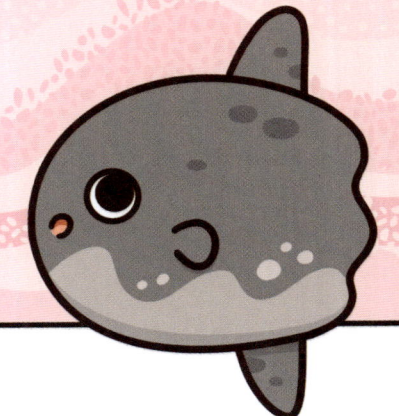

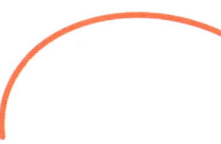

1. Draw a curved line.

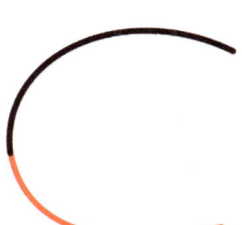

2. Draw a curved line below for the bottom of the head/body.

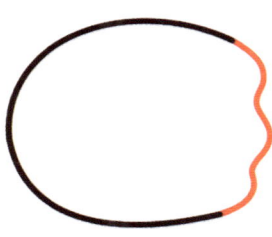

3. Connect the top and bottom of the head/body with a wavy line with three peaks.

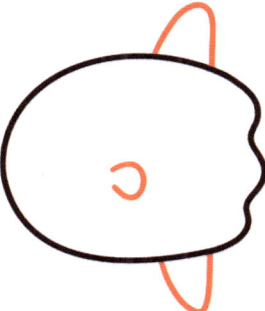

4. Add paddle-like fins on the top and bottom of the body and a backward C fin in the center of the body.

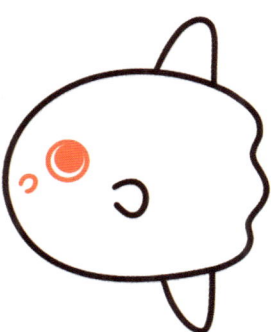

5. Draw a circular eye with a drawn in iris and a small backward C for the mouth. .

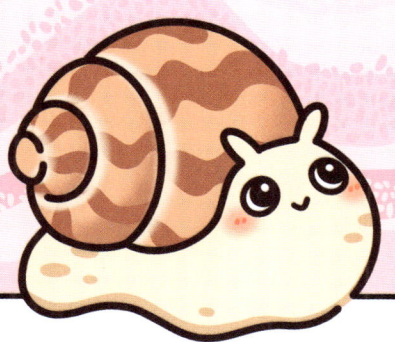

SEA SNAIL

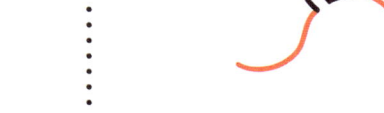

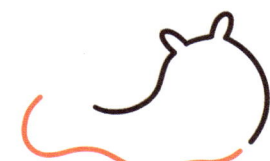

1. Draw two antennae connected by a short line.

2. Draw a semicircle on one side for the face and a curved line for the start of the body on the other side.

3. Draw a wavy line along the bottom with an upturned end.

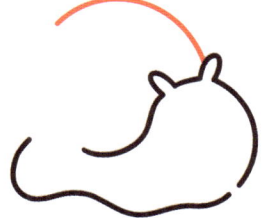

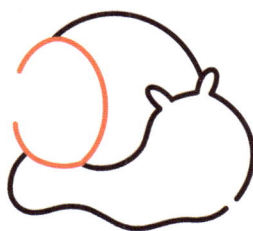

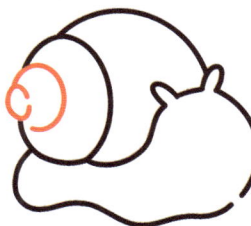

4. Add a curved line over the head.

5. Add an open-ended egg shape at the back of the body.

6. Draw a smaller egg shape on the left of the bigger egg with an even smaller egg shape inside.

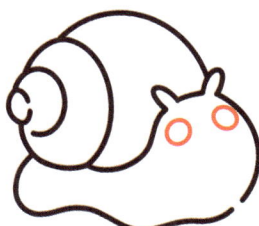

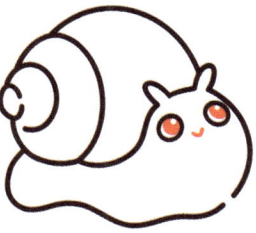

7. Draw two circles below each of the antennae for the eyes.

8. Finish by almost completely filling in the eyes with the irises, leaving white for pupils, and add a small smile in between.

DRESSED TO IMPRESS

Why the gold star?
Because I'm so bright!

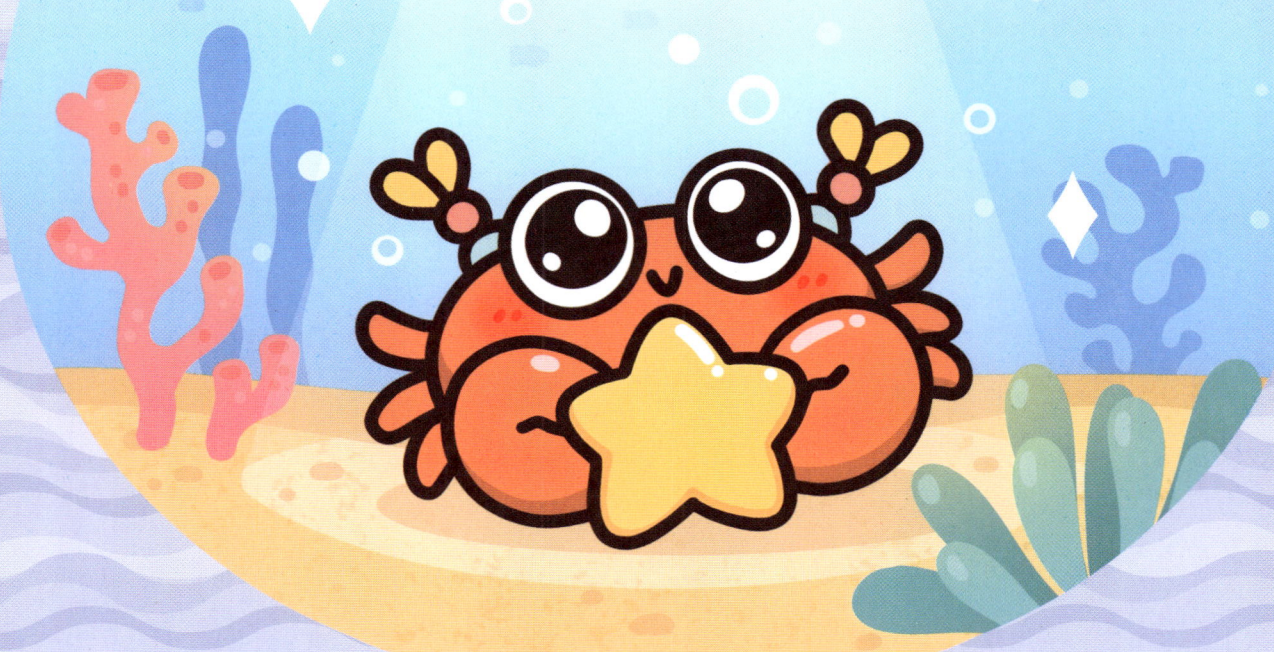

SUPER TUNA

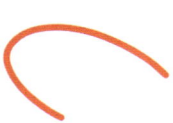

1. Draw one half of an oval at an angle.

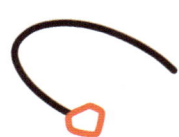

2. Attach a pentagon to the end of the open oval.

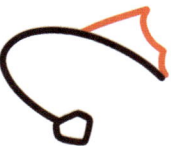

3. Draw a fin with two points and two swoops in between.

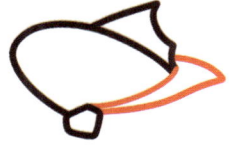

4. Add a triangular scarf shape beneath the head.

5. Draw a curved square beneath the triangular shape for the cape.

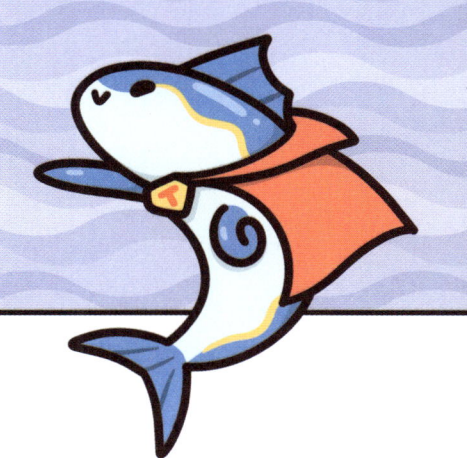

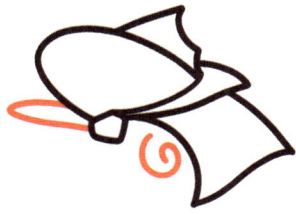

6. Add a rounded arm next to the face and a swirl beneath the pentagon.

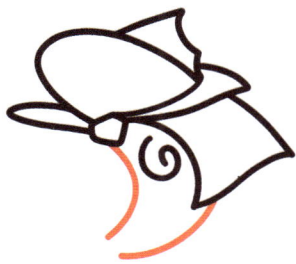

7. Add a curved line connected to the pentagon and also one connected to the cape, convening toward the end of the body.

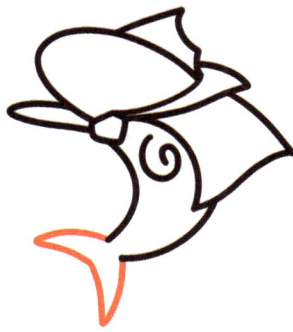

8. Draw a forked tail.

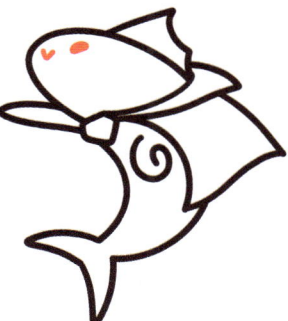

9. Finish with a bean-shaped eye and a small smile.

SAILOR PRAWN

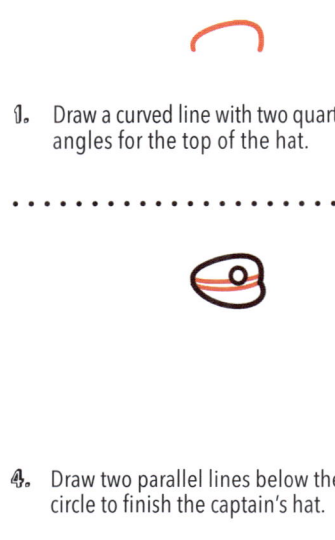

1. Draw a curved line with two quarter angles for the top of the hat.

2. Connect a semicircle below.

3. Add a circle in the middle.

4. Draw two parallel lines below the circle to finish the captain's hat.

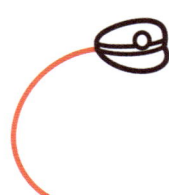

5. Add a semicircle to the left of the hat.

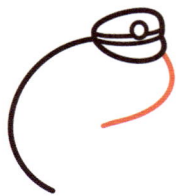

6. Draw a curved line below the hat for the face.

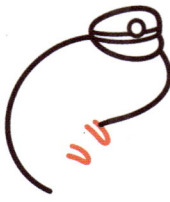

7. Add two small arms below the face.

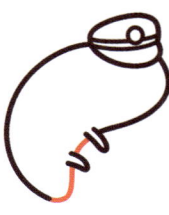

8. Connect the face to the bottom of the body with a curved line.

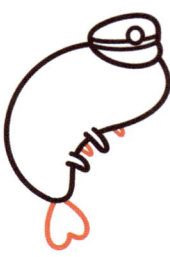

9. Add two smaller arms behind the body and an upside-down heart at the bottom of the body for a tail.

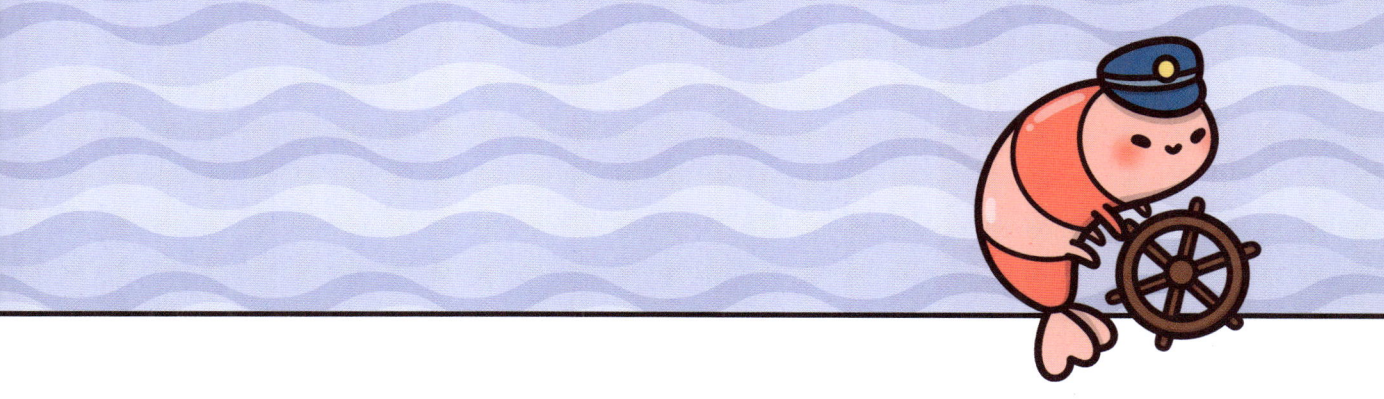

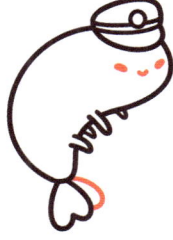

10. Draw bean-shaped eyes and a small smile in between. Add a curved line to the tail.

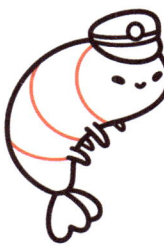

11. Draw three curved lines on the body.

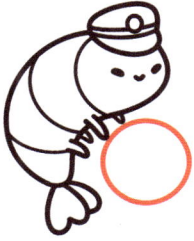

12. Draw a circle at the ends of the prawn's arms.

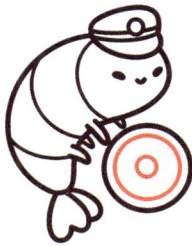

13. Draw two more circles inside the circle.

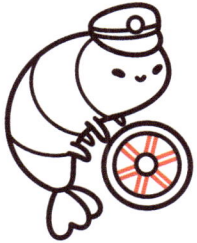

14. Add six double lines around the innermost circle to make the spokes of the wheel.

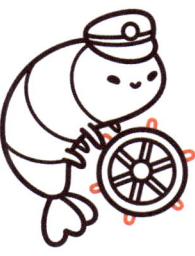

15. Finish by adding the rounded edges to each spoke to complete the wheel.

FROG WIZARD

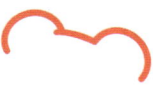

1. Draw two semicircles connected by a curved line.

2. Draw two curved lines on either side of the eyes.

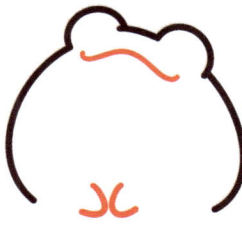

3. Add a curved smile and U-shaped hands at an angle at the bottom of the body.

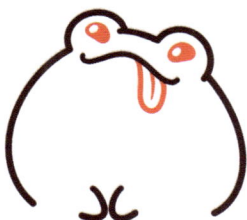

4. Draw bean-shaped eyes, leaving white for pupils, and add a tongue hanging out of the mouth.

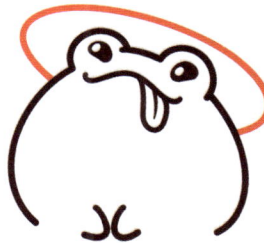

5. Draw an oval through the head/body and above the eyes.

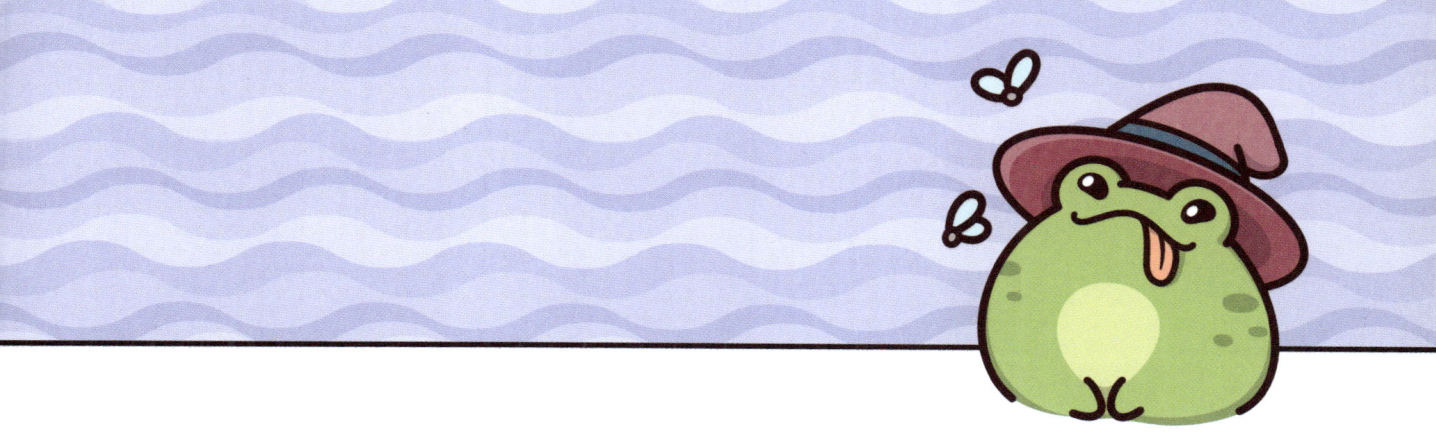

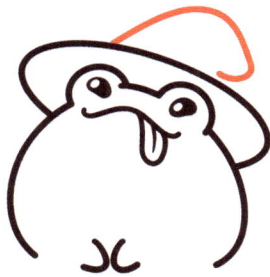

6. Connect a curved line that turns at the end near the oval.

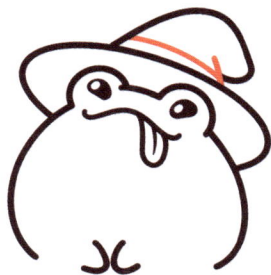

7. Draw a line just above the oval with a sharp turn at the end to close out the hat shape.

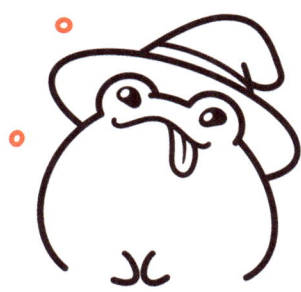

8. Add small circles beside the frog.

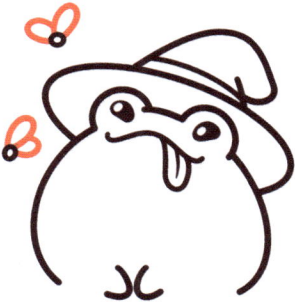

9. Finish with two wings on each circle to make flies.

OTTER'S FAVORITE ROCK

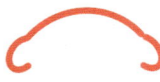

1. Draw a curved line connecting sideways U-shapes for the ears.

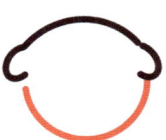

2. Draw a semicircle below to finish the head.

3. Draw three curved lines in a row like a cloud above the head.

4. Draw two curved lines in a row like a cloud below the head to close the flower shape.

5. Add curved lines beneath the flower on either side for the body.

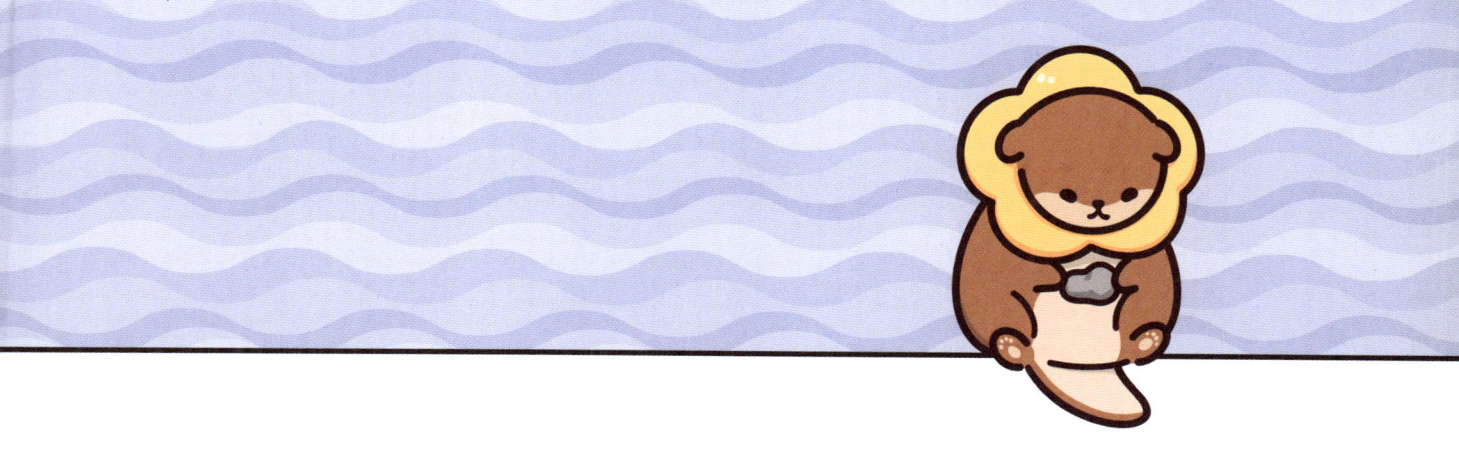

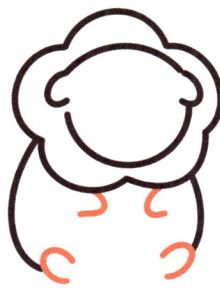

6. Draw C-shaped arms below the head facing in and C-shaped feet on the bottom of the body facing out.

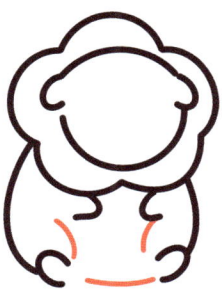

7. Add short, curved lines above the feet for the legs. Draw a short, curved line at the bottom of the body to close the shape.

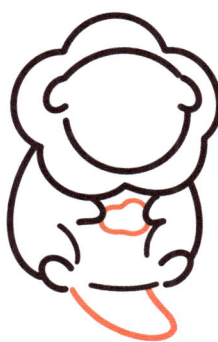

8. Draw a paddle-like tail coming out from the bottom of the body and a roughly circular shape in the otter's hands.

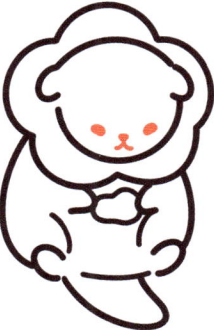

9. Finish with bean-shaped eyes and a small, upside-down triangular nose connected to an upside-down V.

CIRCUS DOLPHIN

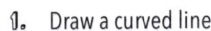

1. Draw a curved line.

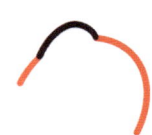

2. Draw a straight line to the left and another, longer curved line to the right.

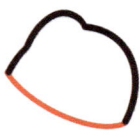

3. Connect the sides with a curved line.

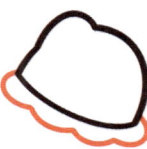

4. Draw a series of curved lines around the bottom of the head.

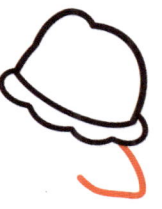

5. Add a pointed fin to the right.

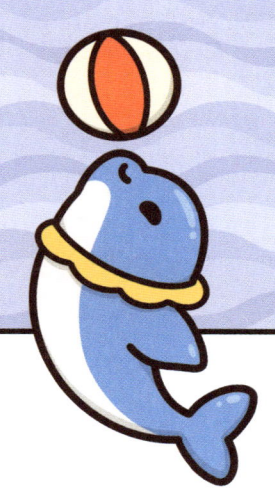

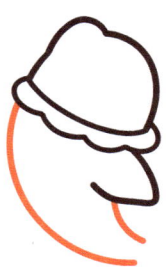

6. Draw two curved lines leading to the end of the body, with the left side longer than the right.

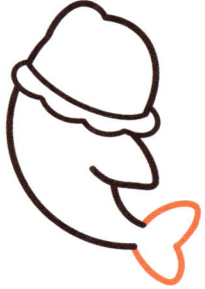

7. Draw a forked tail at the end of the body.

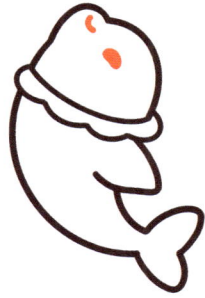

8. Draw a sideways smile on the snout. Draw a bean-shaped eye below the smile.

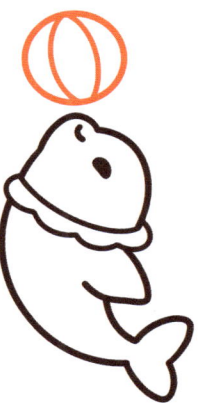

9. Finish with a circle above the snout with two curved lines inside for the ball.

NURSE GARRA RUFA

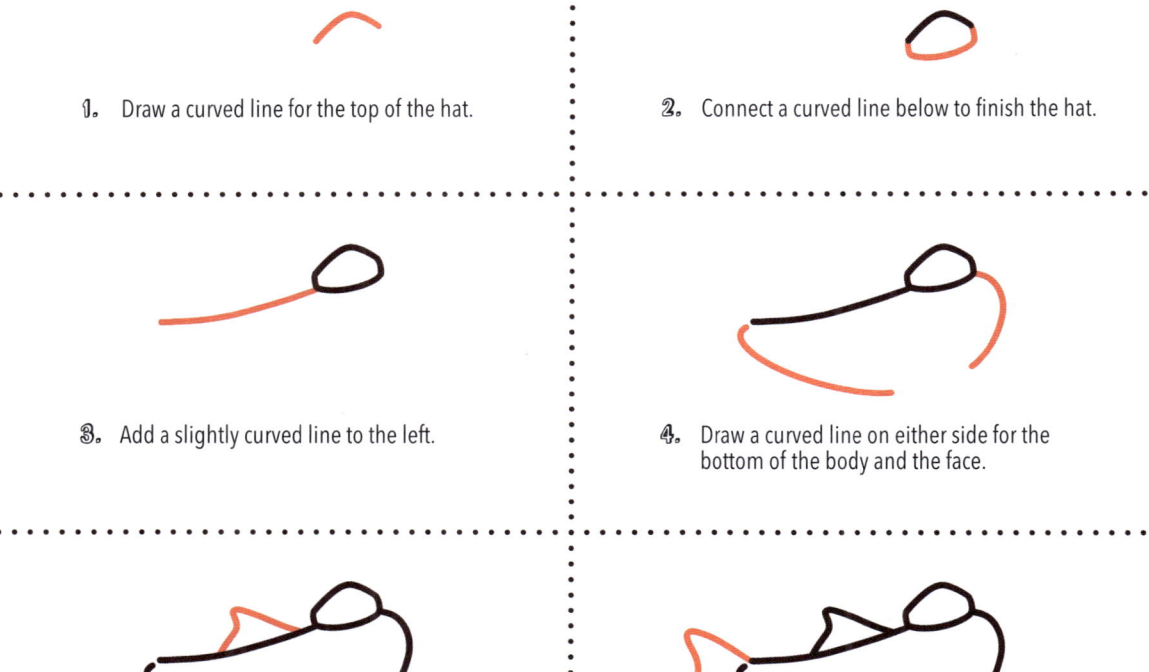

1. Draw a curved line for the top of the hat.

2. Connect a curved line below to finish the hat.

3. Add a slightly curved line to the left.

4. Draw a curved line on either side for the bottom of the body and the face.

5. Add a pointed fin to the top of the body.

6. Draw a forked tail.

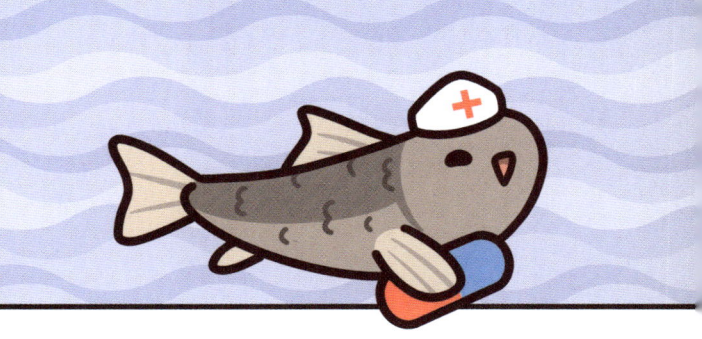

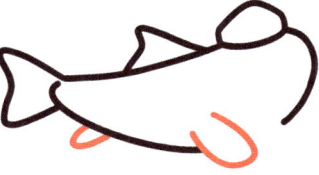

7. Draw a paddle-like fin on the bottom of the body and another small fin just before the tail.

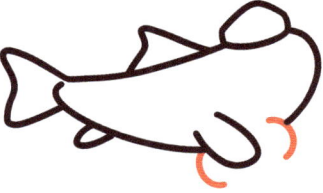

8. Draw two curved lines like parentheses around the front fin.

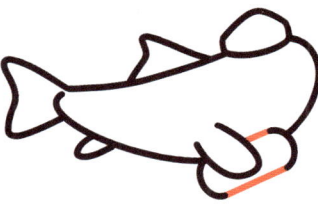

9. Connect the parentheses with straight lines.

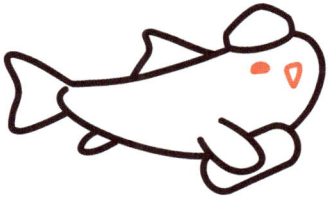

10. Finish with a bean-shaped eye and an open-mouthed smile.

SUPERSTAR CRAB

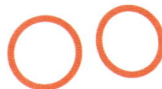

1. Draw two circles side by side for the eyes.

2. Fill in the eyes with round irises, leaving white for pupils and shine.

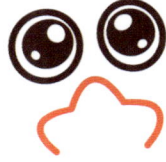

3. Draw the top three points of a star below the eyes.

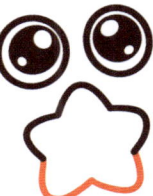

4. Add the bottom two points of the star.

5. Draw two incomplete circles on either side of the star.

6. Draw a jagged line in the center of each incomplete circle to finish the claws. Add a small smile between the eyes.

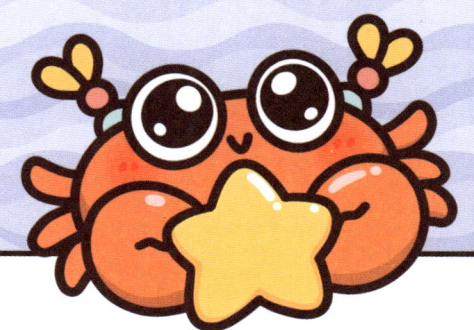

7. Draw the body by connecting the eyes and adding curved lines from the eyes to the claws.

8. Add one leg on each side of the body and a semicircle beside each eye.

9. Draw another leg below each of the first legs and a circle above each of the semicircles beside the eyes.

10. Finish with the last legs below the others and add double loops at the ends of the circles like little wings.

DIVER CROCODILE

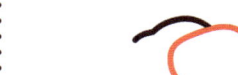

1. Draw a curved line with a bump on one end.

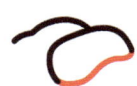

2. Add a staple-like line.

3. Close the staple line with a wavy line.

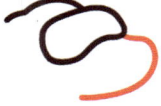

4. Draw the curved line of the snout.

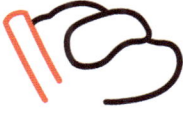

5. Draw parallel lines next to the face, and connect the top ends with a curved line.

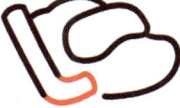

6. Extend the parallel lines with curved lines toward the mouth, and connect the ends with a curved line.

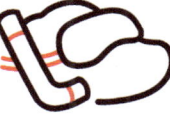

7. Add a lines near the top and bottom of the straw. Draw the parallel lines of the goggle strap around the head.

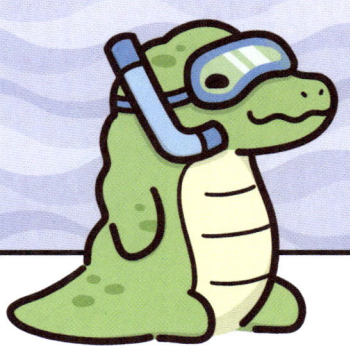

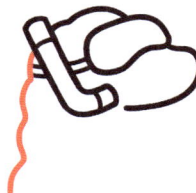

8. Draw the ridged body with four curved lines in a row.

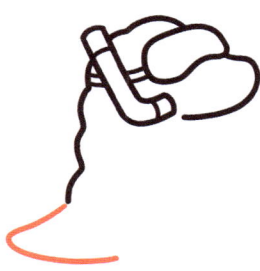

9. Draw the curved line of the tail at the bottom of the body.

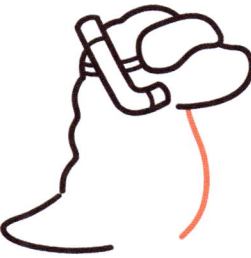

10. Draw the curved line of the stomach beneath the snout.

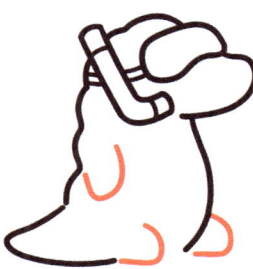

11. Add two backward Cs beside the tail and the stomach for the feet. Draw a U-shaped arm on the left side of the body.

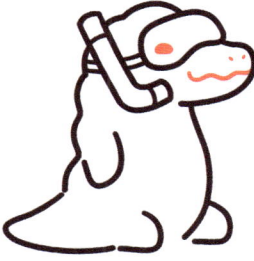

12. Draw the face with a bean-shaped eye in the goggles, two dots on the snout for a nose, and a squiggly line on the snout for a sharp smile.

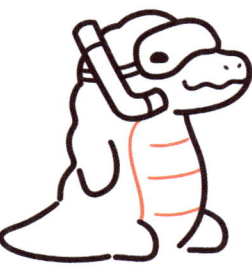

13. Finish with lines on the stomach. Draw a line from the straw to the left foot, and add three horizonal lines across the stomach.

MERMAID MANATEE

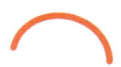

1. Draw a semicircle.

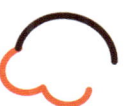

2. Connect a sideways three to the semicircle for the mouth.

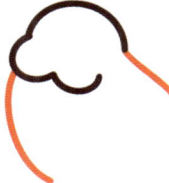

3. Draw a straight line on the right side of the head and a curved line below the face.

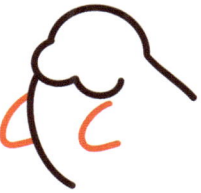

4. Add two C-shaped fins beside the stomach and below the mouth.

5. Draw a curvy line across the midpoint of the body.

6. Draw another curvy line below the other, connecting the two at a point on the stomach side.

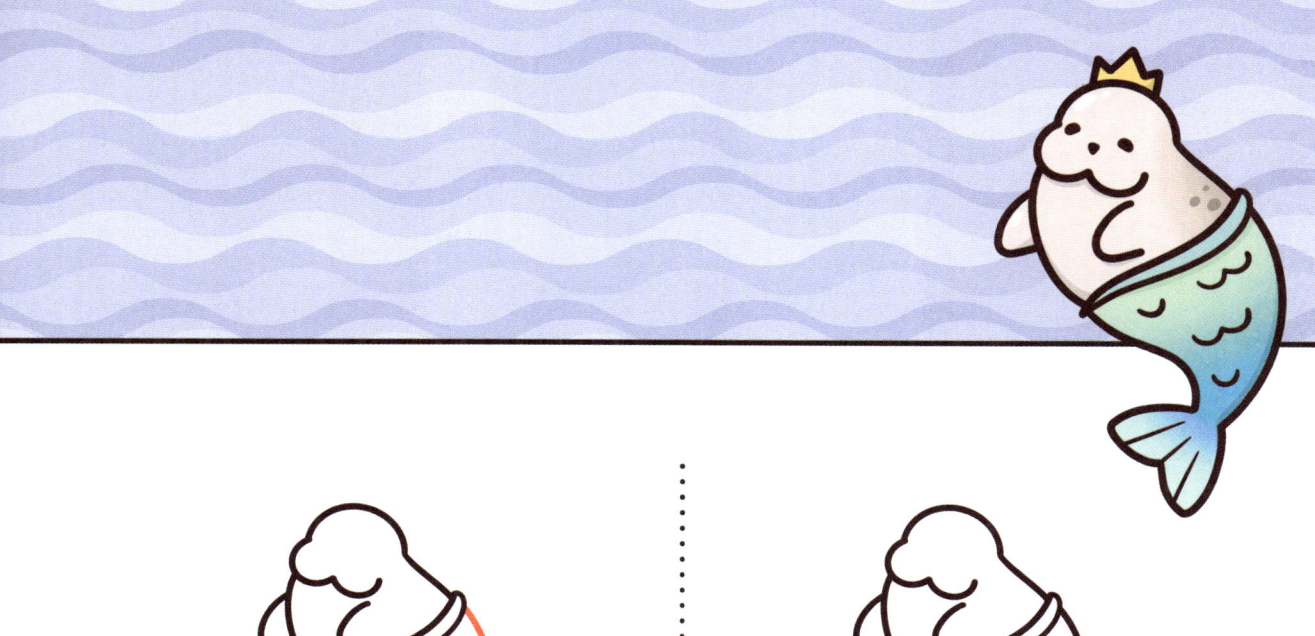

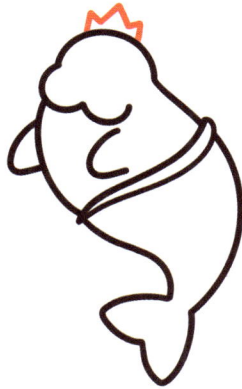

7. Draw the curved sides of the tail almost meeting together at the end.

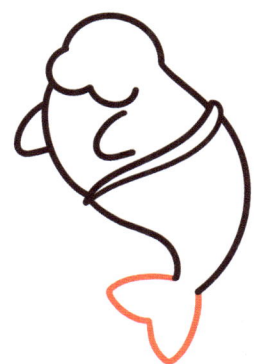

8. Add the forked tail.

9. Draw a three-pointed crown on top of the head.

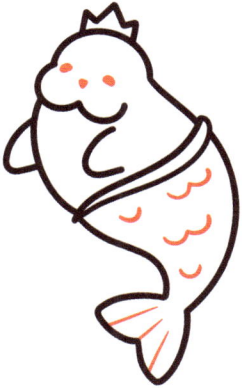

10. Finish with bean-shaped eyes, a triangle-shaped nose, U- and sideways E-shaped scales on the tail, and lines on the tail for texture.

MORAY EEL REAPER

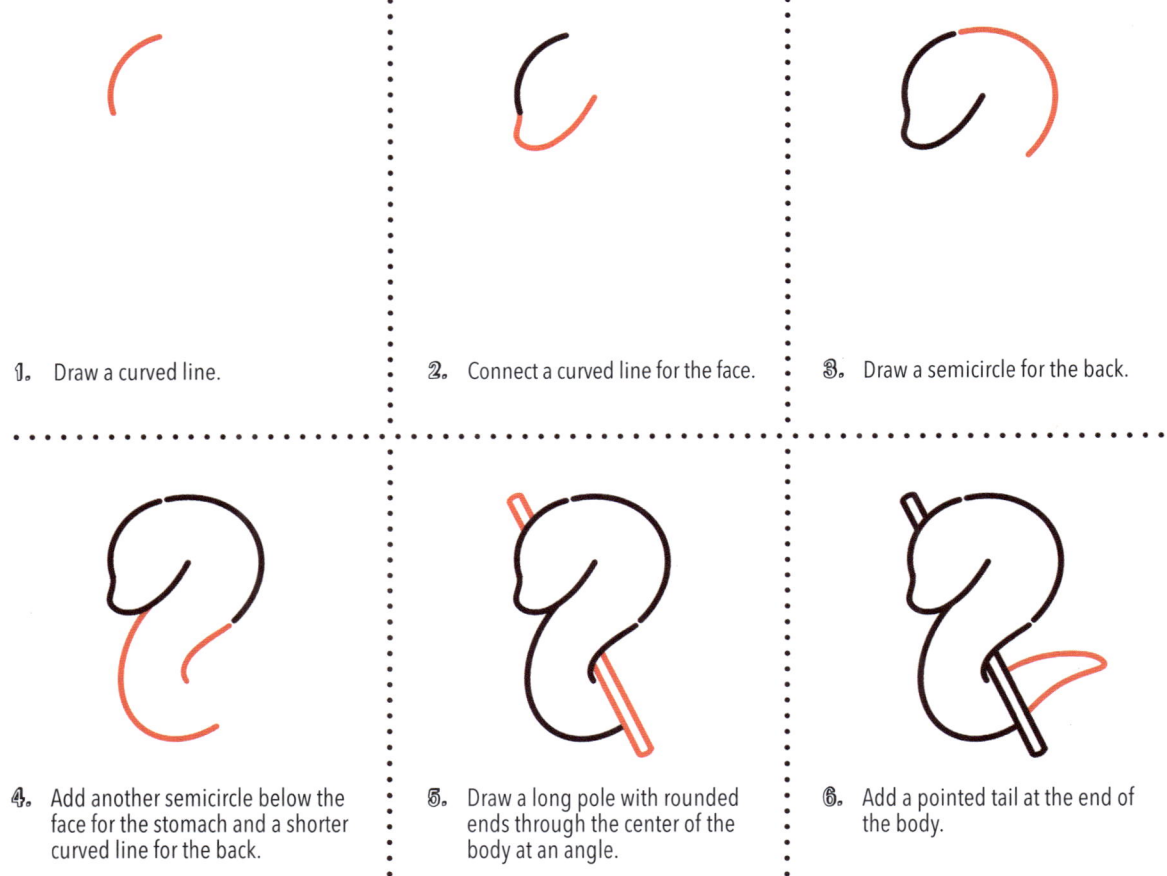

1. Draw a curved line.

2. Connect a curved line for the face.

3. Draw a semicircle for the back.

4. Add another semicircle below the face for the stomach and a shorter curved line for the back.

5. Draw a long pole with rounded ends through the center of the body at an angle.

6. Add a pointed tail at the end of the body.

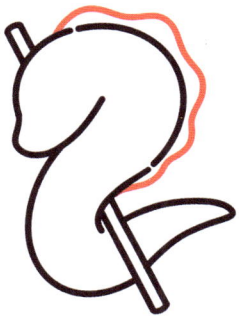

7. Add a wavy fin from the center of the head to the middle of the body.

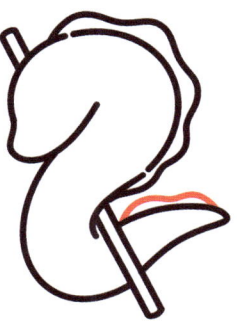

8. Add another wavy fin along the tail.

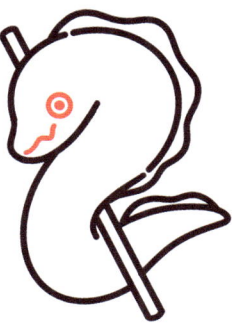

9. Draw the eye with a circle and dot inside it and a line with a sharp tooth for the mouth.

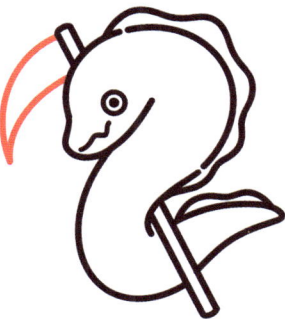

10. Finish by drawing the curved, pointed blade of the scythe.

HABITAT DIRECTORY

Here's a handy directory to find out where in the world your favorite sea creatures live. It's organized by saltwater (ocean) and freshwater (lakes & rivers) bodies of water. Land and coastal animals can often be found on the forest line along lakes and rivers and sometimes

Ocean

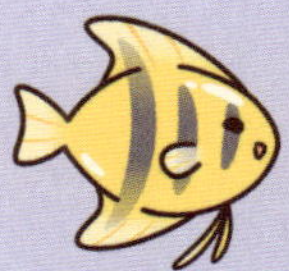

Angelfish	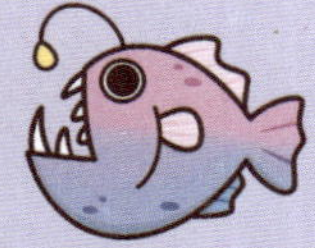 Anglerfish	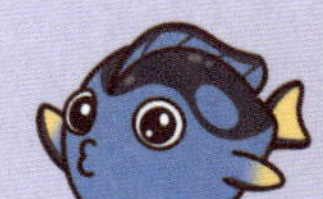 Blue Tang	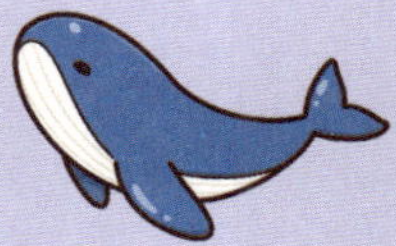 Blue Whale	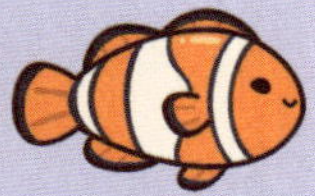 Clownfish
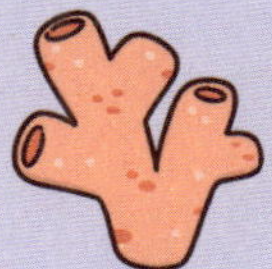 Coral	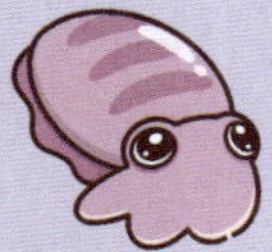 Cuttlefish	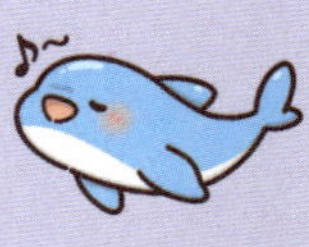 Dolphin	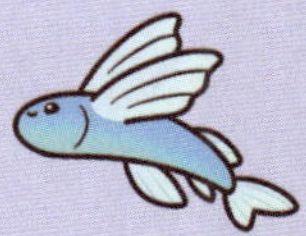 Flying Fish	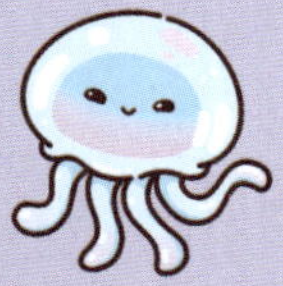 Jellyfish
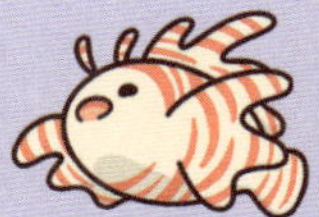 Lionfish	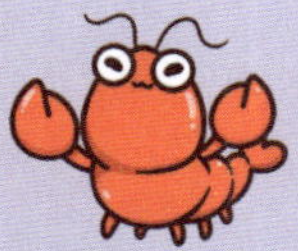 Lobster	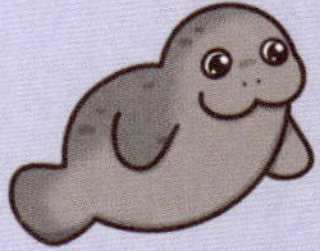 Manatee	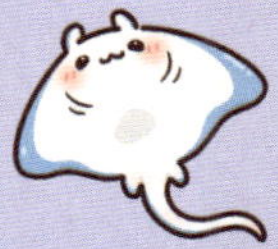 Manta Ray	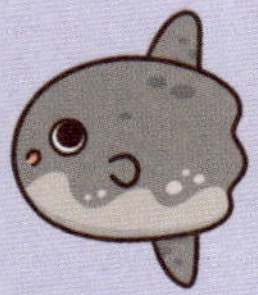 Mola
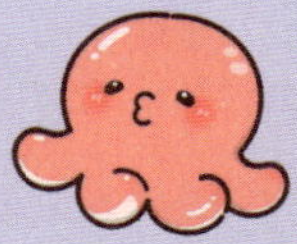 Octopus	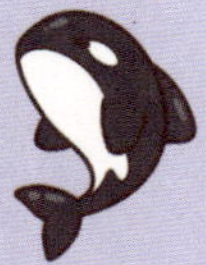 Orca	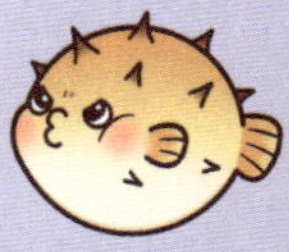 Pufferfish	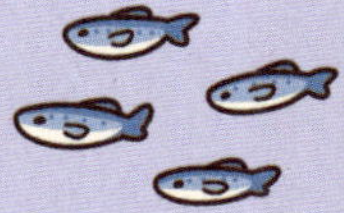 Sardines	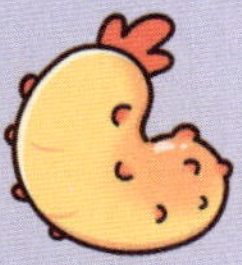 Sea Cucumber
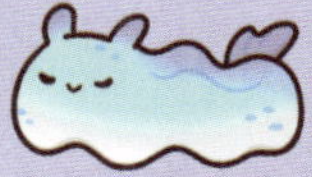 Sea Slug	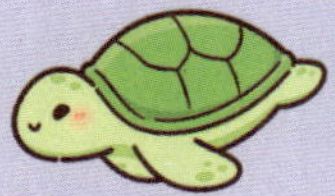 Sea Turtle	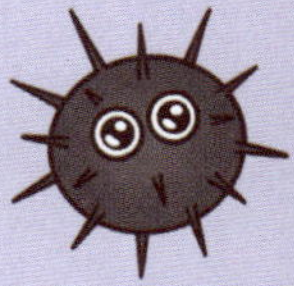 Sea Urchin	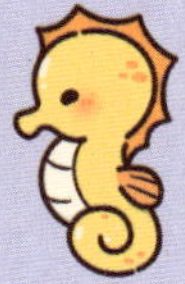 Seahorse	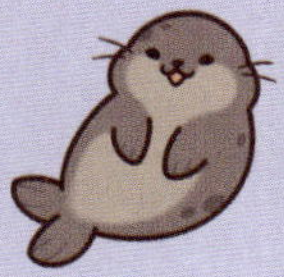 Seal
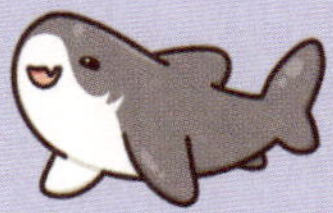 Sharks	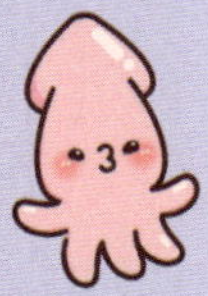 Squid	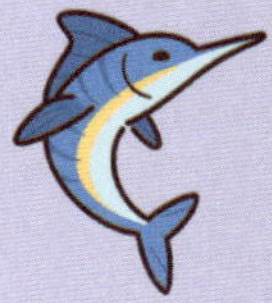 Swordfish	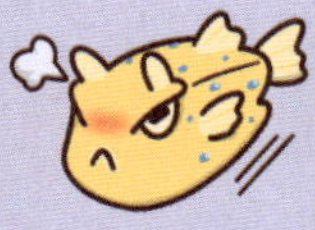 Thornback Cowfish	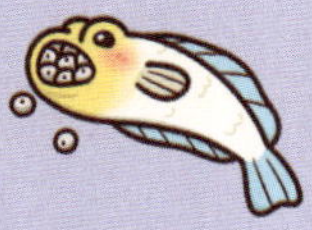 Yellowhead Jawfish

on the beach in tide pools—shallow pools of seawater that form on the rocky shore. Some creatures, like angelfish, live in both salt water and fresh water. Wherever in the world they are, they're born to swim!

Lakes & Rivers

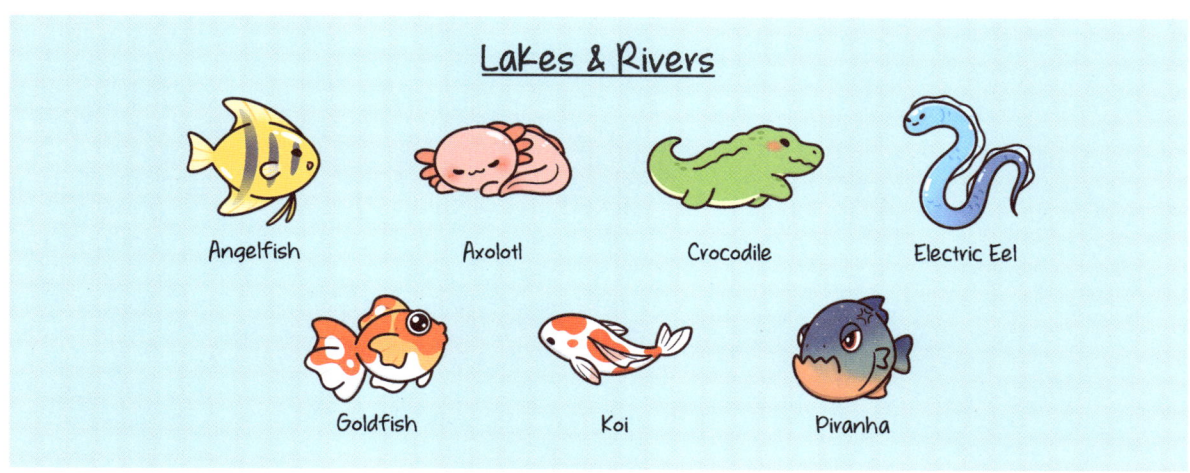

Angelfish · Axolotl · Crocodile · Electric Eel

Goldfish · Koi · Piranha

Land & Coast

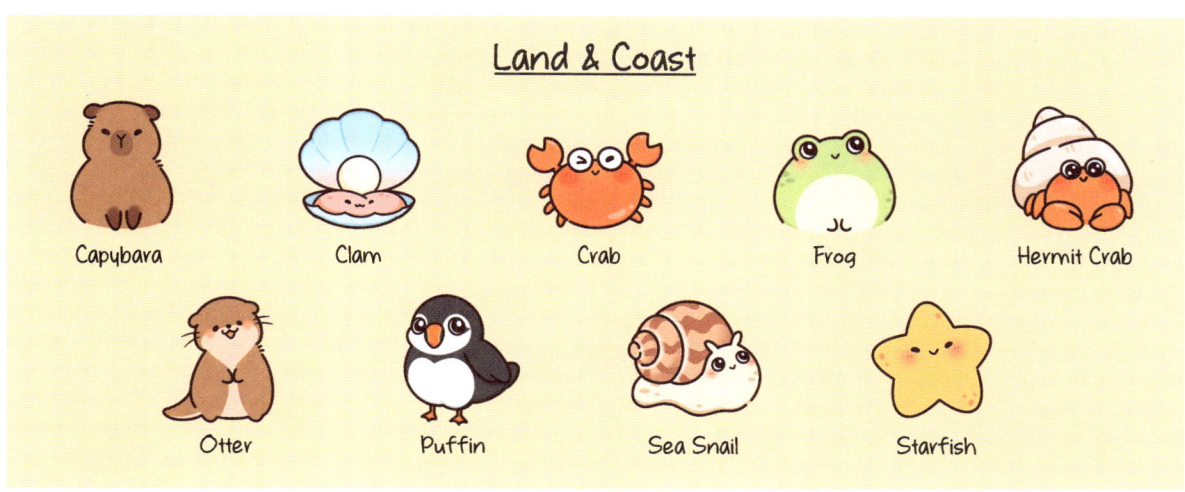

Capybara · Clam · Crab · Frog · Hermit Crab

Otter · Puffin · Sea Snail · Starfish

North & South Pole

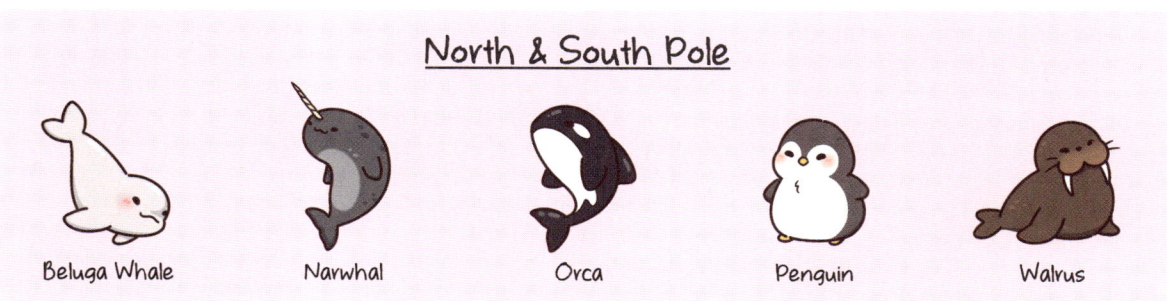

Beluga Whale · Narwhal · Orca · Penguin · Walrus

COLORING PAGES

Wait, there's more! Have fun coloring, adding patterns, decorating, or even accessorizing the sea creatures on these pages. You can follow the color palette on pages 14-15 and pattern inspiration on page 11, or be original. It's up to you!

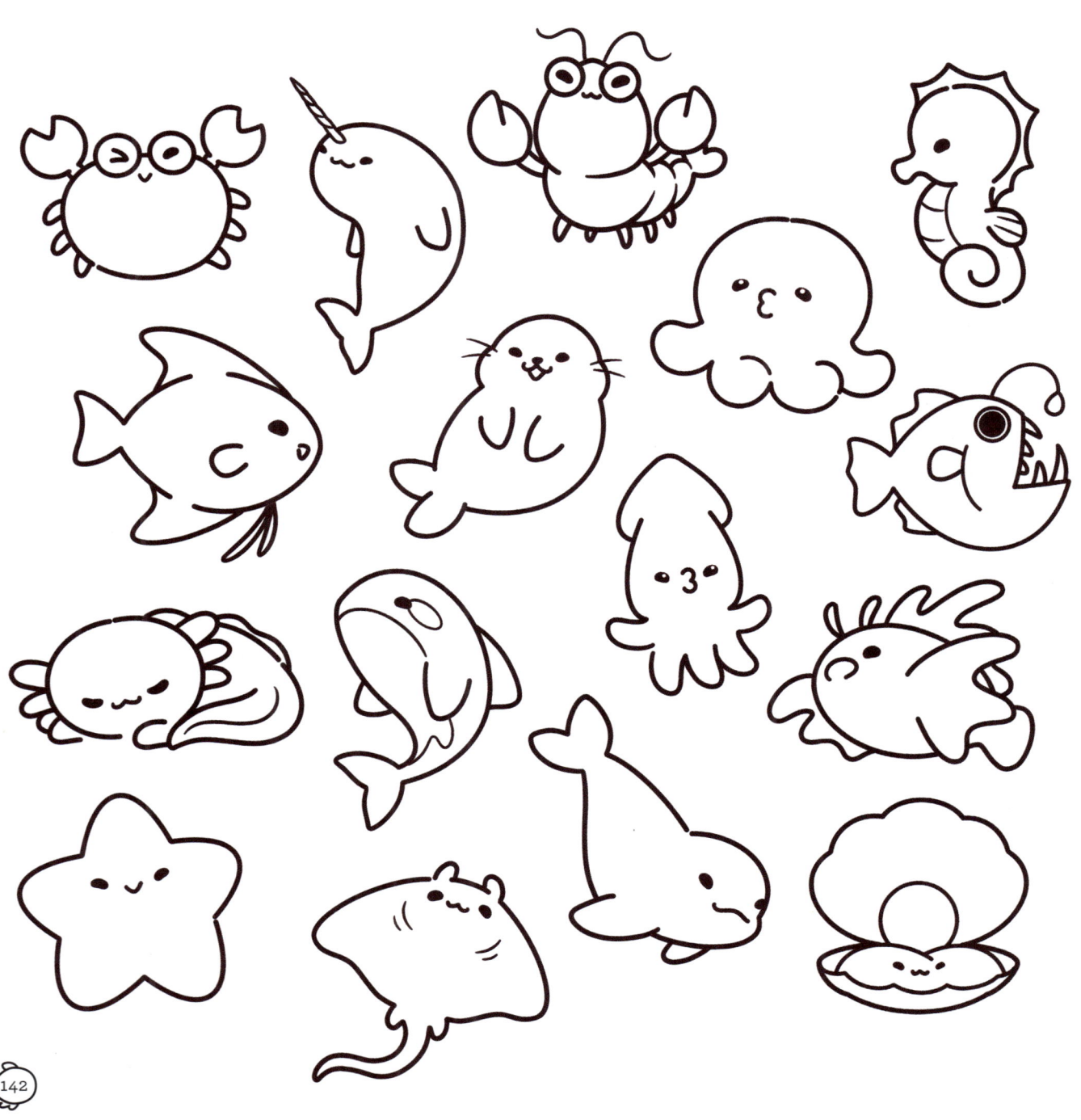

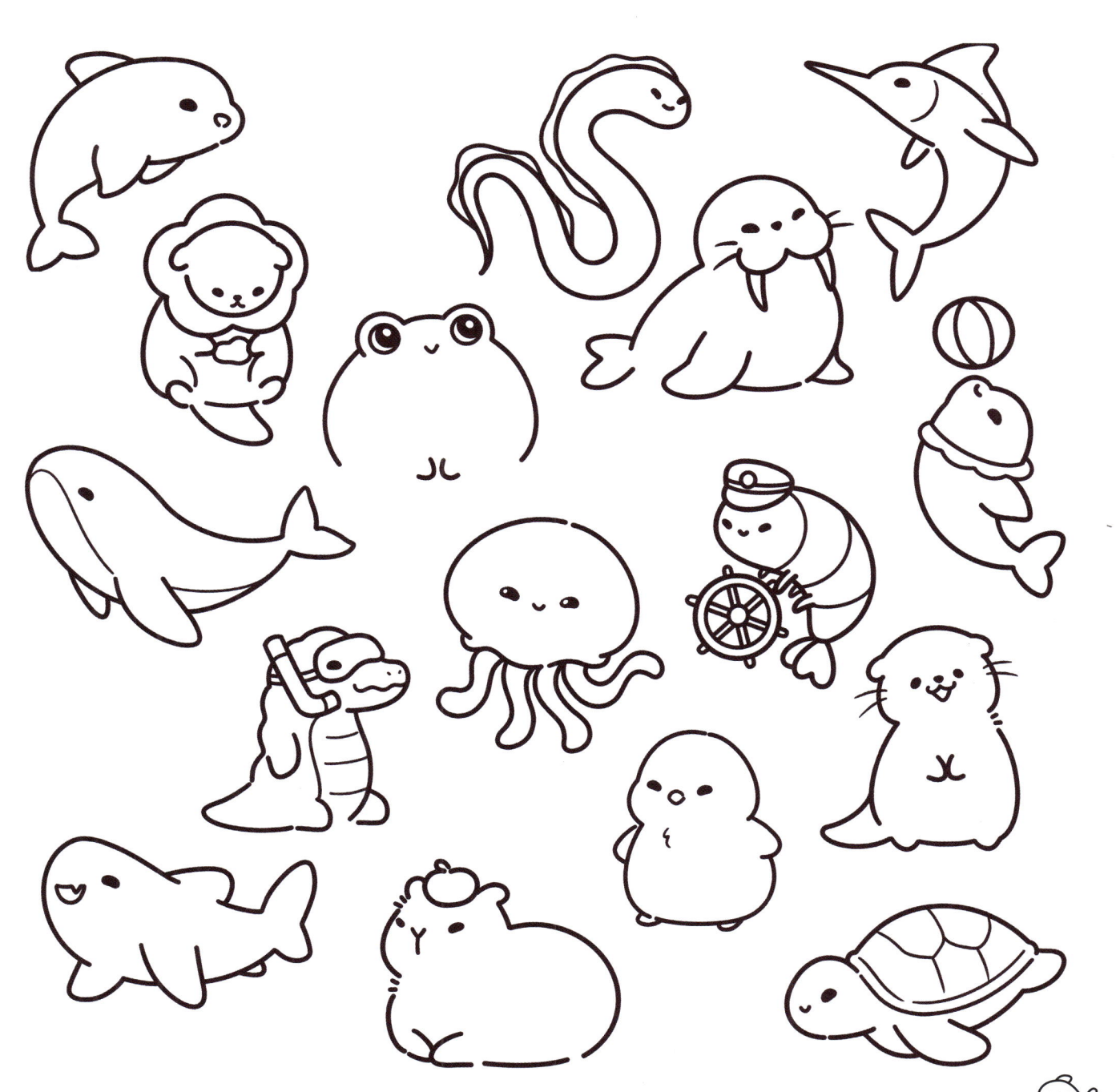

Acknowledgments

Throughout this journey, I've gained invaluable insights and faced both triumphs and challenges. There have been times of feeling overwhelmed, yet the drive to create keeps me moving forward. I extend heartfelt gratitude to my Niko Studio cofounder, Wee Lim, for his hard work, and to my creative team at Niko Studio for their dedication in growing the Bichi Mao brand. To everyone who has shown love and support over the past five years, thank-you immensely. Your encouragement has been invaluable, and I'm committed to continuing this journey, spreading joy and creativity along the way.

About the Author

Olive Yong is a self-taught artist from Malaysia. Drawing has always been a passion of hers, but it was in June 2019 that she first ventured into digital art. She began sharing her creations across social media under the brand name Bichi Mao, never expecting this humble start to lead to such incredible opportunities.

Bichi Mao is a slice-of-life webcomic series featuring cat characters illustrated in an adorable art style. Beyond comics, Bichi Mao offers unique collaborations, 3D toys, and merchandise available worldwide. With 2D and 3D animation, the series' goal remains to spread warmth and positivity, making each Bichi Mao tale a cherished experience.

Yong's other books published by The Quarto Group include *Kawaii Kitties: Learn How to Draw 75 Cats in All Their Glory* and *Kawaii Doggies: Learn to Draw 75 Adorable Pups in All Their Glory*. She has also published *Color My Mood: A Cute Activity Journal for Tracking My Feelings* (Union Square & Co.) and two books with a local Malaysian publisher: *Bichi Mao: The Purrfect Moment* and *Bichi Mao: Our Memories*.